4th International Research-to-Practice Conference Lighting Design (LD-2017)

SHS Web of Conferences Volume 43 (2018)

St. Petersburg, Russia
12 – 13 October 2017

Editors:

R. Narboni
A. Bakholdin
M. Fontoynont
N. Bystryantseva

ISBN: 978-1-5108-6200-5

Printed from e-media with permission by:

Curran Associates, Inc.
57 Morehouse Lane
Red Hook, NY 12571

Some format issues inherent in the e-media version may also appear in this print version.

Printed by Curran Associates, Inc. (2018)

For additional information, please contact EDP Sciences – Web of Conferences at the address below.

EDP Sciences – Web of Conferences
17, Avenue du Hoggar
Parc d'Activité de Courtabœuf
BP 112
F-91944 Les Ulis Cedex A
France

Phone: +33 (0) 1 69 18 75 75
Fax: +33 (0) 1 69 28 84 91

contact-edps@webofconferences.org

Additional copies of this publication are available from:

Curran Associates, Inc.
57 Morehouse Lane
Red Hook, NY 12571 USA
Phone: 845-758-0400
Fax: 845-758-2633
Email: curran@proceedings.com
Web: www.proceedings.com

TABLE OF CONTENTS

 https://doi.org/10.1051/shsconf/20184301001

Foreword

Lighting is a technique, it is an art, it is a narrative, it proposes a visual experience which can be shared. It is broad, it is universal. Many professionals contribute to explore and understand further what can be done with light: in physics, medicine, material science, biology, art, architecture, photography, events organisation, etc. It is therefore essential to establish platforms for exchange between these fields. The large scope of contributions in these proceedings demonstrates how broad this could be.

Over more than 100 years, lighting practice has developed with two major objectives: to satisfy basic visual requirements (primarily, for indoor activities) and to guarantee safety of citizens in urban areas (for displacement outdoors at night). This lead to definitions of minimum lighting requirements for lighting installations.

In the pyramid of Maslow which displays the hierarchy of needs (Abraham Maslow, 1943), these two aspects concern the basic fundamental needs related to physiology and safety. The next two layers (belonging, esteem) are other levels of fundamental needs. They are related to the position of the individual in a group. This is where the issue of identity becomes essential. Identity is a fundamental need.

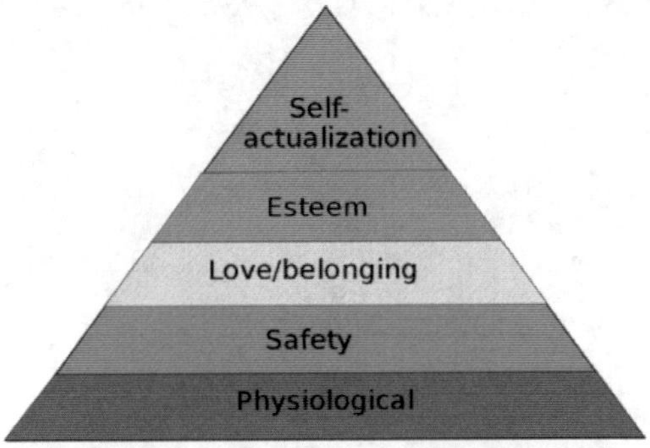

Fig. 1. Maslow Hierarchy of Needs (1943).

But identity is both an individual need and a social need.

As an individual need, we need to establish a link with our origin, with our environment, with the place we were born, with our climate, etc.

As a social need, we need to relate to our family, our friends, our city, our country, or cultural history, any value we share and cherish.

It is important to note that images and more specifically lighting are the important elements of this identity. One can mention, for example, religious and non-religious festivities with candles, or light constructions (Christmas trees, Christmas decorations, fireworks, candles placed on a windowsill in Lyon, France during La Fête des Lumières every year on the 8th of December, etc.).

Cities play a significant role in social identity. With the development of electric light during the XXth century, street candelabra became significant elements of urban identity of a city. After 1960, with the development of high power arc lamps, lighting techniques expressed, at nighttime, facades, bridges, and monuments, thus, enhancing the character of places of importance for the inhabitants and the visitors. Later, with dynamic lighting and video display, new "immaterial" approaches became common.

Fig. 2. Church of Savior on Spilled Blood in St Petersburg, an essential element of the city's nightscape.

Fig. 3. New York Time square, with dynamic displays.

Fig. 4. Las Vegas Strip, with powerful animated lighting effects.

However, other, more subtle ways to express identities of places with light exist. For example, Copenhagen urban lighting offers a subtle balance between light produced by the luminaires hanging above the streets, and the wall lamps next to building entrances.

Fig. 5. Hanging lamps in Copenhagen streets.

Lighting strengthens the character of a city, it can also propose new events, which progressively become part of a city identity, such as the rotating light on the top of the Eiffel Tower in Paris, which is an add-on effect of a landmark that creates an "immaterial" landmark.

Fig. 6. Rotating projector on the top of the Eiffel Tower in Paris.

Lighting can definitely contribute to the identity of a city. But what is most important is that it contributes to strengthening the relations between citizens and their place, as well as visual memories of visitors.

By proposing a conference on "Identity through the Light Environment", the organizers aimed to address the extraordinary potential of light for narration – i.e: production of scientific, artistic or emotional content. Lighting is a modern tool, and new digital lighting technologies are offering new possibilities to analyse or develop our relation to the luminous environment. This will create new opportunities which are largely discussed in the following papers. Contributions are from a broad domain, and they demonstrate benefits of the interdisciplinary approach.

We hope you will find inspiration in this document.

Prof. Marc Fontoynont
Department of Energy Performance, Indoor Environment and Sustainability of Buildings
Danish Building Research Institute, Aalborg University, Denmark

edp sciences

Web of Conferences

Statement of Peer review

In submitting conference proceedings to *Web of Conferences*, the editors of the proceedings certify to the Publisher that

1. They adhere to its **Policy on Publishing Integrity** in order to safeguard good scientific practice in publishing.
2. All articles have been subjected to peer review administered by the proceedings editors.
3. Reviews have been conducted by expert referees, who have been requested to provide unbiased and constructive comments aimed, whenever possible, at improving the work.
4. Proceedings editors have taken all reasonable steps to ensure the quality of the materials they publish and their decision to accept or reject a paper for publication has been based only on the merits of the work and the relevance to the journal.

Title, date and place of the conference

The 4th International Research-to-Practice Conference Lighting Design – 2017 (LD-2017)
12-13 October 2017, The New Stage of Alexandrinsky Theatre, St. Petersburg, Russia

Proceedings editor(s): Aleksei Bakholdin

Date and editor's signature 01 03 2018

edp sciences

Web of Conferences

Statement of Peer review

In submitting conference proceedings to *Web of Conferences*, the editors of the proceedings certify to the Publisher that

1. They adhere to its **Policy on Publishing Integrity** in order to safeguard good scientific practice in publishing.
2. All articles have been subjected to peer review administered by the proceedings editors.
3. Reviews have been conducted by expert referees, who have been requested to provide unbiased and constructive comments aimed, whenever possible, at improving the work.
4. Proceedings editors have taken all reasonable steps to ensure the quality of the materials they publish and their decision to accept or reject a paper for publication has been based only on the merits of the work and the relevance to the journal.

Title, date and place of the conference

The 4th International Research-to-Practice Conference Lighting Design – 2017 (LD-2017)
12-13 October 2017, The New Stage of Alexandrinsky Theatre, St. Petersburg, Russia

Proceedings editor(s): Marc FONTOYNONT

Date and editor's signature 15-02-2018

edp sciences

Web of Conferences

Statement of Peer review

In submitting conference proceedings to *Web of Conferences*, the editors of the proceedings certify to the Publisher that

1. They adhere to its **Policy on Publishing Integrity** in order to safeguard good scientific practice in publishing.
2. All articles have been subjected to peer review administered by the proceedings editors.
3. Reviews have been conducted by expert referees, who have been requested to provide unbiased and constructive comments aimed, whenever possible, at improving the work.
4. Proceedings editors have taken all reasonable steps to ensure the quality of the materials they publish and their decision to accept or reject a paper for publication has been based only on the merits of the work and the relevance to the journal.

Title, date and place of the conference

The 4th International Research-to-Practice Conference Lighting Design – 2017 (LD-2017)
12-13 October 2017, The New Stage of Alexandrinsky Theatre, St. Petersburg, Russia

Proceedings editor(s): Natalia Bystryautseva

Date and editor's signature 13.02.2018г

edp sciences

Web of Conferences

Statement of Peer review

In submitting conference proceedings to *Web of Conferences*, the editors of the proceedings certify to the Publisher that

1. They adhere to its **Policy on Publishing Integrity** in order to safeguard good scientific practice in publishing.
2. All articles have been subjected to peer review administered by the proceedings editors.
3. Reviews have been conducted by expert referees, who have been requested to provide unbiased and constructive comments aimed, whenever possible, at improving the work.
4. Proceedings editors have taken all reasonable steps to ensure the quality of the materials they publish and their decision to accept or reject a paper for publication has been based only on the merits of the work and the relevance to the journal.

Title, date and place of the conference

The 4th International Research-to-Practice Conference Lighting Design – 2017 (LD-2017)
12-13 October 2017, The New Stage of Alexandrinsky Theatre, St. Petersburg, Russia

Proceedings editor(s):

Roger Narboni

Date and editor's signature ROGER NARBONI

January the 22nd, 2018

Real-time, anthropomorphic 3-D scanning and voxel display system using consumer depth cameras as an interactive means of individual artistic expression through light

Andrei-Ducu Predescu[1] and *Georgios Triantafyllidis*[1]

[1]AAU Copenhagen, Department of Architecture Design and Media Technology, 2450 A.C Meyer Vænge 15, Copenhagen SV, Denmark

Abstract. The research presented in this paper revolves around the development of an interactive light installation called NEO-David. The focus is on the development of kinetic light within the boundaries of real-time generated anthropomorphic form. The case study seeks to address the issues related to democratic aspects of art and participatory artistic development. The paper presents the setup of such a system and explores different technical development challenges of the design.

1 Introduction

The paper aims to establish a theoretical framework for the development of a system capable of recreating three-dimensional properties of an individual within the boundaries of a three-dimensional display area. Furthermore, the system's goal is to create real time content as opposed to already available pre-generated information. The paper describes the research, development methodology and prototyping procedure of the NEO-David light art installation, which main goal is the development of a possibility in representing an anthropomorphic abstraction of an individual, while at the same time being capable of "mirroring" the movement generated by the user interacting with the installation.

1.1 Concept

The idea behind the installation is based on an architectural concept known as the Musicon Masterplan Development. The flagship element of the masterplan is represented by the Ragnarock Museum for Pop, Rock and Youth Culture. The museum has tried to embody the metaphor of a rockstar's lifestyle [1]. However, certain elements of this metaphor have not managed to survive the cruel reality of budget austerity. The NEO-David Installation aimed to be a conceptual prosthesis, trying to complete the original concept idea. The NEO-David has thus become part of the architectural ensemble by providing support in "celebrating" the individuals coming to visit the Ragnarock Museum; hence, conceptually, it tries to mimic the attention given by the public to the "rockstar". By creating a sculptural element that takes the average individual and transposes her or him to a "stage" that gratifies and offers a temporary axis-mundi status to everyone, the conceptual red thread of the Ragnarock regains wholesomeness and strengthens the idea of democratic space and freedom of expression within the overall Musicon Masterplan identity.

1.2 Theoretical development

To develop a system that is capable of reproducing a real-time, three-dimensional animated model, we need to first understand the capabilities of today's scanning technologies. One of the most accessible products on the market with such capabilities is the Kinect, device, classified as a motion sensor input device. Originally developed by Microsoft in 2010, as a means of interaction with the XBOX 360 gaming platform, it has been quickly embraced by the MAKER community and open source software was developed to access the data generated by this device. [2]

The Kinect can generate a point cloud of the environment it "sees", which, through processing, can later be translated into a real-time tree-dimensional model of the environment. However, the generated model is an incomplete representation of the environment, having numerous artefacts as well as occlusion issues, where the device is incapable of detecting surfaces. The major issue with using one device lies in the fact that the generated model is not a full three-dimensional object, but it is more similar to a classical relief. Hence, even though the model can update real-time it is incapable of generating a fully three-dimensional output that can later be used to populate a three-dimensional display area. However, this paper will try to address this issue through theoretical means.

The second part of the project has to deal with the display area of the model. In order to understand what the output methodology will be we firstly have to grasp how an object manifests itself within physical space. An object found in the physical or digital realms presents itself as a compact collection of voxels. Each of these individual voxels has a series of properties, such as dimension and a coordinate system relative to its world coordinates. An accumulation of voxels results in the generation of a form. Using basic geometric principles, we can generate a form through the appropriate distribution of voxels which can be directly translated within a display area, which has identical voxel representation parameters, such as voxel size and spacing of the composing elements. [3]

2 Design

Recreating the form of an individual through light is a complex issue, mainly having to do with the voxel resolution of the form. When dealing with the visual perception of a form, experimentation regarding the appropriate spacing of the voxel arrays is critical. After this first step has been completed, considerations for the spatial qualities of the installations have to be investigated. Lastly, the scanning area has to be established and the software dealing with compilation of the individual cloud points and merger into one continuous three-dimensional model has to be developed.

2.1 Spatial properties

Having to deal with the human body as an interaction element, the installation area has to be able to accommodate the physical dimension and interaction space, which is within the physical grasp of an individual.

The Modulor is one of the most well-known studies in the field of design. Developed by a Swiss-French architect Corbusier, it proposes a unifying scale between the imperial and metric system by adopting a methodology which implies using the human body as a means to impose scale upon objects and spaces. Even though in many ways it is a system that could seem obsolete or outdated, it has a significant advantage, having as a basis a highly humanistic approach to design, while also putting the individual at the centre of rationalisation as opposed to an aleatory mechanical like establishment of dimensions. [4]

Based on this investigation, it was concluded that the optimal spatial properties of the installation, which are able to accommodate a large range of the movement manifested through the anthropomorphic form generated, are as follows: a height of 2.26m, a width of 2.26m and a depth of 1.13m, as shown in Figure 1. [4]

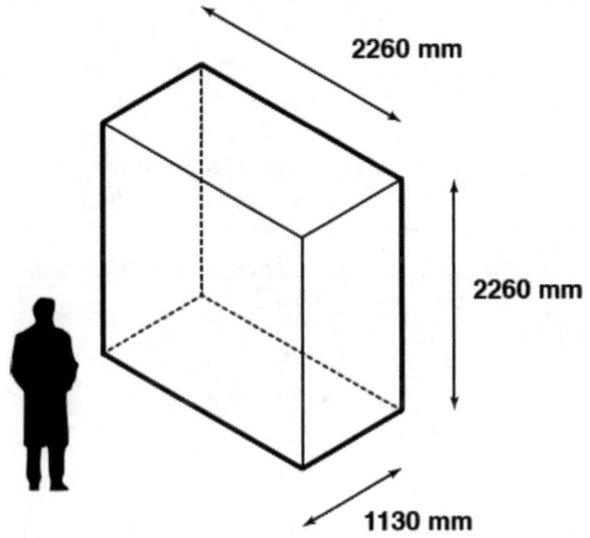

Fig. 1. Spatial properties of the display area and its relative size to an average size individual.

The interaction and scanning zone also needs to be able to facilitate the room required for individuals to interact with the installation as well as allowing for non-users to transit the area. Three scanning pillars are placed in around the area in order to form an equilateral triangle, measuring 4.75m between the posts. In the centre of this perceived triangle lies the actual interaction, as shown in Figure 2.

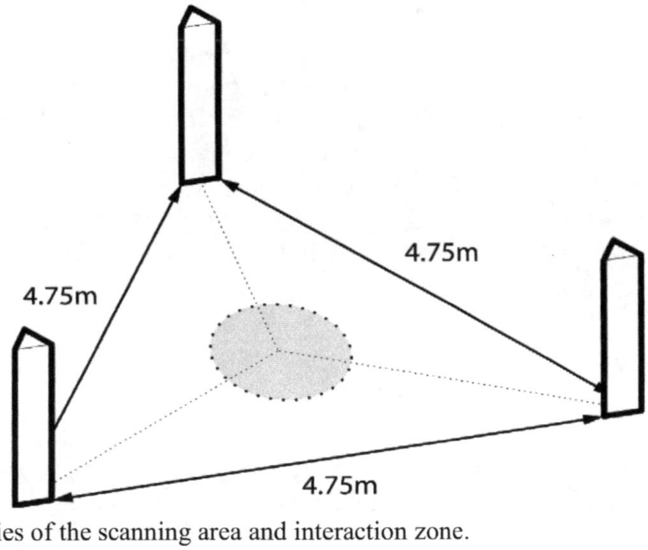

Fig. 2. Spatial properties of the scanning area and interaction zone.

2.2 Scanning area and technological principles

As mentioned before, a system capable of registering the 3D has to be put in place to develop a fully three-dimensional real-time model.

As such this system needs to be capable of not only registering this data but also compiling it into our desired output. In order to cover the 360 degrees around a model, a minimum of 3 scanning devices have to be used. Furthermore, each device needs to cover an area of minimum 130 degrees of the scanned model. This ensures an overlapping area between the three different surfaces, which helps in processing the date to a continuous 3D model. [5]

A software dealing with this intense computational process of patching together a 3D model from several sources must be populated with relevant information, such as the exact position of the scanning devices and the spatial relation between the three elements as well as the individual cloud point generated by each of them. Each individual cloud point brings a unique set of data to the system; however, as mentioned before, to create the fully three-dimensional model, the "overlapping" area between the different cloud points is critical. The reference position of each individual scanning device coupled with the "overlap" helps ensure a minimum of errors. The "overlap" establishes a bridging area between the cloud points; by comparing the different position between two points which are supposed to have an identical xyz coordinate, the software can compute the necessary adjustments. To identify which points from the different "clouds" correspond to each other, , the colour information of each voxel is compared to further ensure accuracy on top of the corresponding position approximation.

2.3 Display Area

The internal matrix structure will also be dimensioned according to the proportions coming from Le Corbusier's system. In order for the vision of the spectator to penetrate the matrix, so that he or she could easily understand the recreated shape, an appropriate spacing between the light pods needs to be take into consideration. As discussed above, the higher the density of the matrix is, the more accurate the physical representation of the form we obtain. However, as the elements become more and more compact, the problem of self-obstruction becomes a critical issue.

To solve this problem, a series of tests are necessary to establish the optimal spacing. Using a sequence or distances, relating to the Modulor, has led to a conclusion that a grid spacing of 48 mm could be the most optimal distance for our intended purposes. [4]

Because of this arrangement, the matrix will contain 48.668 LEDs, meaning that if all light sources were to be turned on, they would have a total power consumption of approx. 4.000 W/H and a total luminous intensity of 83.000 cd. However, such a scenario will never occur, most likely the maximum number of LEDs that will be active when a user is interacting with the installation will be around 4.500.

3 Prototype

The development of a working prototype has been a priority from the very first moment of the project idea, having in mind both proving that the technology required to achieve the desired outcome already exists and identifying any potential design flaws. It has also been a way of understanding the intricacies of the project, varying from the physical properties of the "medium" in the installation to the phenomenology of the anthropomorphic representation, which is unveiled using light.

3.1 Prototype development

Through intensive experimentation the prototype has allowed for establishing the principles that have further improved the final design in efficiency, through the development of possible construction technics, power supply methods, data transmission protocols and software engineering.

The prototype has been a key element in revealing the physicality of this work, both from an artistic perspective and as a logistic exercise. Despite a certain "mechanical" look, the installation is softened by the gentle light effects playfully moving within its domain.

The physical prototype was developed using the knowledge acquired at the initial digital experimentation stage, as well as the through the use of additional components, which could not be tested until this point. In order to achieve a fully working scale partial model of the sculpture, we needed to incorporate the additional components of the installation, such as a control system for the matrix, a scanning method and a power supply fitting the energy requirements of the prototype.

For the intended purpose of creating a proof-of-concept prototype, the control system was aligned to a standard PC, used in running the developed software, coupled with a FadeCandy micro-controller, which is able to output the computed data to the LED matrix. FadeCandy is the perfect tool for creating interactive light setups when using addressable LEDs. Being an open source hardware means that its Open Pixel Control protocol is compatible with many existing general high-level programming languages. The Fadecandy controller can drive up to 512LEDs, arranged in eight strips of up to 64 LEDs connected to a laptop through a USB port. [6]

To scan our environment, we will be using the Kinect standard. However, for the purpose of demonstration, the prototype only applies two of these devices, as opposed to the three used by the full-scale sculpture.

The matrix will be composed out of 512 PL9823 F5 RGB LEDs arranged in eight grids of 8x8 LEDs with a spacing of 48mm, which, when stacked on top of each other, result in a cubic lattice with a dimension of 35x35x35cm. This particular LED has a high data transmission stability and is able to receive and forward large information package output. It is able to produce luminous intensity up to 2000 mcd using 5v 20mA. This product has a very good performance and a long lifespan. [7]

The large number of LEDs require the appropriate power supply running at a low voltage. The lighting elements need supply that is able to provide the required current. As each individual LED needs 20mA per colour channel, a quick calculation reveals that in order to fully power the entire matrix at maximum brightness, we would need an electric source able to deliver 5V with a minimum of 40A.

3.2 Conceptual software prototype

One of the most challenging aspects in developing the prototype related to the development of the software driving the installation. It is an initial building block for a fully functional algorithm that can recreate a real time 3D representation. As discussed above, the prototype used only two Kinect, meaning that the computed data was incomplete. To transmit the data to the display area, the main idea behind the algorithm developed was to slice this representation to individual plates.

By using the OPC library within the Processing development environment, we were able to create an algorithm that uses the FadeCandy micro controller in order to address the appropriate Voxel (Pixel/LED) within the 3D Matrix of LED. For this purpose, , the model was sliced at eight different levels of depth; the outline was defined, and the shape was filled with a chosen colour.

The OPC library cannot work with voxels, only with pixels; therefore, the slices had to be converted into a two-dimensional plane to allow data collection, thus sending data to the variable “collector”. The 512 collectors were spread out evenly on the surface coinciding with the screen space. [8]

3.2 Unifying Multiple Cloud Point Coordinates

The individual cloud points were generated using two Kinect sensors and the openKinect library for Processing. The library was developed as an open source tool for the exploratory applications of these sensors.

By using the RawDepth arrays generated by the library, we are able to translate the points to the Cartesian system using the following nested for loop.

```
for (int x = 0; x < Kinect.width; x ++)
for (int y = 0; y < Kinect.height; y ++)
int offset = x + y*640
int rawDepth = newDepth[offset]
Vector v = depthToWorld(x, y, rawDepth)
```

The depthToWorld functions performs the necessary computations for the points displayed in the appropriate 3D position. It deals with the internal calibration parameters of the sensors. [9]

Once the cloud points had been generated, attention had to paid to how the two relate to each other and what parameters are needed for their alignment and generation of the third cloud point containing the unified data.

In physics and engineering, Davenport chained rotations are three chained intrinsic rotations about body-fixed specific axes. Euler rotations and Tait–Bryan rotations are the cases of the Davenport general rotation decomposition. The angles of rotation are called Davenport angles because the general problem of decomposing a rotation in a sequence of three was studied first by Paul B. Davenport. [10]

This means that each vertex in the cloud point needs to be rotated in 3D space in order to create a unified coordinate system. In this convention Roll1 imposes the "heading", Pitch is the "inclination" (complementary of the elevation), and Roll2 imposes the “tilt”. The matrixes that are needed for multiplication are as follows:

$$R_z(\phi) = \mathrm{Roll}_1(\phi) = \begin{bmatrix} \cos\phi & -\sin\phi & 0 \\ \sin\phi & \cos\phi & 0 \\ 0 & 0 & 1 \end{bmatrix}$$

$$R_y(\theta) = \mathrm{Pitch}(\theta) = \begin{bmatrix} \cos\theta & 0 & -\sin\theta \\ 0 & 1 & 0 \\ \sin\theta & 0 & \cos\theta \end{bmatrix}$$

$$R_z(\psi) = \mathrm{Roll}_2(\psi) = \begin{bmatrix} \cos\psi & -\sin\psi & 0 \\ \sin\psi & \cos\psi & 0 \\ 0 & 0 & 1 \end{bmatrix}.$$

Following the calculation of the matrix multiplication, they had to be translated into the new coordinate system to create the unified cloud point. The origin of matrix multiplications is always a fixed point. Nevertheless, there is a common workaround using homogeneous coordinates to represent a translation of a vector space with matrix multiplication: Write the 3-dimensional vector $\boldsymbol{w} = (wx, wy, wz)$ using 4 homogeneous coordinates as $\boldsymbol{w} = (wx, wy, wz, 1)$. [11]

To translate the individual cloud points, each homogeneous vector *p* contained within the matrix can be multiplied by the vector *v* (describing the position of each Kinect sensor) using the following translation matrix:

$$T_{\mathbf{v}} = \begin{bmatrix} 1 & 0 & 0 & v_x \\ 0 & 1 & 0 & v_y \\ 0 & 0 & 1 & v_z \\ 0 & 0 & 0 & 1 \end{bmatrix}$$

Thus, the multiplication will show the expected result as described below:

$$T_{\mathbf{v}}\mathbf{p} = \begin{bmatrix} 1 & 0 & 0 & v_x \\ 0 & 1 & 0 & v_y \\ 0 & 0 & 1 & v_z \\ 0 & 0 & 0 & 1 \end{bmatrix} \begin{bmatrix} p_x \\ p_y \\ p_z \\ 1 \end{bmatrix} = \begin{bmatrix} p_x + v_x \\ p_y + v_y \\ p_z + v_z \\ 1 \end{bmatrix} = \mathbf{p} + \mathbf{v}$$

Through the process described above, we can generate a continuous cloud point, which can be displayed with the domain of the physical installation. hence, creating a system that can generate real-time content as well as displaying it in three dimensions.

3 Conclusion

Following the development of the prototype, several conclusions can be made regarding the areas investigated. While developing the prototype, it has proven to be very challenging to assembly the display area. The process required to develop the individual plates of LEDs has proven to be extremely time consuming. Should this not be the case of the prototype, this aspect could have been avoided by involving manufacturers that can produce the LED sheets according to the design specifications.

The most challenging part of the experiment, as in a method of rationalising 3D space, was related to the development of the software prototype. Even though it was simplified in order to better understand the intricacies of generating a 360 degrees 3D model, the software development is a crucial part for the further advancement of the system. It appears that previous efforts in this field, such as the development of the NOVA system, were confronted with the same problems. However, previous systems dealt with pre-generated and not real-time content. [12]

Previous research in the field of real-time 3D data reconstruction has been done by different research groups. The most promising research results are presented in the following paper: "Real-Time, Full 3-D Reconstruction of Moving Foreground Objects From Multiple Consumer Depth Cameras" [13]. However, this study does not address the output aspect of data or any potential artistic implications of the technology.

The research in the representation of form and movement through light is far from being exhaustive; however, the initial experimentation has proven to be extremely promising. Further research and development of the software is needed to make this concept a reality.

References

1. MVRD and COBE, Rockmagneten Masterplan, (2016).
2. Zhang W., Microsoft Kinect Sensor and Its Effect. IEEE Multimedia. 19, 4–10 (2012).
3. Foley, James D.; Andries van Dam; John F. Hughes; Steven K. Feiner "Spatial-partitioning representations; Surface detail". Computer Graphics: Principles and Practice, (1990).
4. Cohen, J.-L., Le Corbusier's Modulor and the Debate on Proportion in France. *Architectural Histories (2014 .*

5. Kwan Pang Tsui; Kin Hong Wong; Changling Wang; Ho Chuen Kam; Hing Tuen Yau, et al. " Calibration of multiple Kinect depth sensors for full surface model reconstruction ", *Proc. SPIE* 10011, First International Workshop on Pattern Recognition, 100111H (July 11, 2016).
6. Micha Elizabeth Scott, FadeCandy Data Sheet, (2016).
7. PL9823 F5 RGB, Data Sheet.
8. OLE (Object Linking and Embedding) for Process Control.
9. Daniel Shifman, "Getting Started with Kinect and Processing".
10. P. B. Davenport. "Rotations about nonorthogonal axes." AIAA Journal, Vol. 11, No. 6 (1973).
11. Richard Paul. "Robot manipulators: mathematics, programming, and control: the computer control of robot manipulators", MIT Press Cambridge (1981).
12. Schubiger-Banz S., Eberle M. The NOVA Display System. In: Adams R., Gibson S., Arisona S.M. (eds) Transdisciplinary Digital Art. Sound, Vision and the New Screen. Communications in Computer and Information Science, vol 7. Springer, Berlin, Heidelberg (2008) .
13. Real-Time, Full 3-D Reconstruction of Moving Foreground Objects From Multiple Consumer Depth Cameras, IEEE, Transactions on Multimedia Volume: 15, (2013).

Interactive lighting art installation in virtual environments as a stimulus for public Ownership in urban development – Brighter Brunnshög

Boa Kim[1*], *Emmanouil* Xylakis[2], and *Georgios* Triantafyllidis[2]

[1]Dept. of Sculpture, College of Fine Arts, Seoul National University, 1 Gwanak-ro, Gwanak-gu, Seoul 08826, South Korea
[2]Dept. of Architecture, Design & Media Technology, Aalborg University Copenhagen A.C. Meyers Vænge 15, 2450 Copenhagen SV, Denmark

Abstract. Urban development projects are often [1]opposed by residents due to a lack of sense of ownership over the project. This study is a methodological approach in creating interactive lighting art installations in virtual environments to stimulate this sense of ownership. The study is part of the Brighter Brunnshög project, which is the initial stage of the urban development plan for new research centres in Brunnshög, Sweden. The main goal of this research is to explore the impact of virtual lighting art installations on residents′ attitudes toward the urban development of their area. The research is based on qualitative field studies and focus group interviews, and was assessed with questionnaires. The design itself is based on the results of the research data and consists of three criteria; awareness, mutuality, and adaptability. The results of the assessment indicate that interactive lighting art installations in virtual environments have the potential to create awareness of areas under urban development, which is a fundamental condition for creating place attachment, and by extension, a sense of ownership over the project.

1 Introduction and motivation

Urban development, which invariably entails construction programs, is often not welcomed by local residents since, for many, it signifies losing a tight-knit location-based community [1]. Despite the possible advantages that come with urban development, losses are weighted more heavily than gains in what is referred to as endowment effect [2]. This aspect and understanding of place and community attachment has become part and parcel of the planning stages of current day urban development projects [3]. As such, planners put in place schemes to encourage continued use of the sites under development where possible, and as such prevent a total detachment and subsequent discontent by the public. To address the fear of loss experienced by the public, it is necessary to support the local sense of heritage, culture, and activities during the construction [4, 5, 6]. These elements of inclusion are subject to requirements relating to time, control and organization. Firstly, for the process to be

* Corresponding author: avo07@snu.ac.kr

successful, the public need to be included for a certain minimum amount of time in each area of the development [4]. Secondly, the public need to have certain control over what Strahilevitz and Loewenstein (1998) call the entity, i.e., the urban development, by using their own system. Finally, self-investment scores highest when these achievements are based on self-organization [6].

The above-mentioned three conditions have been argued by Van Dyne, Pierce, Vandewalle & Kostova to relate directly to attachment, and in extension of this, a sense of psychological ownership over the area [7, 8]. Since these conditions imply that attachment cannot be moved from one place to another, and since the physical aspects of the space to which they are attached will change significantly, an alternative platform must be found which represents their routines, and which maintains their sense of heritage as the site transforms. This point of attachment and ownership can be addressed by using an interactive lighting installation based on an art-design approach.

With the urban development initiative Brighter Brunnshog from energy firm Kraftringen as an example, I will argue for the use of an interactive lighting installation in a virtual environment representing the area under development, to promote a sense of ownership by local residents over urban development projects, and as such promote a positive attitude towards the development of the area.

2 An example project – Brighter Brunnshög

Brunnshög, an area northeast of Lund, Sweden, consists mainly of farmland and has a population of around 14.000. The urban development of the area is projected to increase the population to around 40.000, and include the development of new infrastructure and transportation networks. The urban development is substantial, and Lund's municipality has started the construction of a residential area, a science park, and a research centre housing the world's biggest electron microscope. While construction is well underway for the science village, the residential area and the research centre, two sections remain untouched: a small section of woodland including a conservation protected area, and a section used for local community-based activities, including a small forest with willow huts. The current users of the area are residents and workers in nearby towns such as Norra Faläden, Ideon Science Park and Lund itself.

The Brighter Brunnshög project, run by the Swedish energy firm Kraftringen, forms an important public relations part of the urban development of the area, and as such, is responsible for both informing the residents about the project, and ensuring positive feedback. The proposal to use artistic lighting design as a tool to maintain a smooth transition for the residents and users of the area falls under its auspice.

The study consists of two parts: firstly, the design development of the interactive art installation based on field studies and end-user research, and secondly, the process of creating the virtual environment, the virtual installation with its lighting, and the interactive system that connects the site, the installation and the users. The evaluation within this research is aimed at understanding the psychological impact of the virtual installation on people's attitudes within Kraftringen´s Brighter Brunnshög project, and assessing its potential as a tool to reduce the alienation felt by residents in urban development projects.

3 Related studies

3.1 Art and design: abstraction and factum

Although the primary parameter of the installation would be to maintain a sense of public ownership over the urban development of the area, the design and content of the installation must be based on anthropological studies and methodologies. However, an installation faces two challenges stemming from the differences between design and art. Any design is fundamentally factual and instrumental in nature, rather than abstracting [9]. On the other hand, the aspect of abstraction is an equally important parameter of the installation; i.e., the installation must present in abstract form the continued connection and heritage of the public after their site has physically changed. Rather than design, abstraction requires art [9]. Art can stimulate personal imagination and appeal to the subconscious. However, it relies heavily on the artist's personal understanding, and as such may lack the insight to understand the public and the space it is situated in. This understanding is critical if one is to create a sense of ownership over an urban development project in which both the public and its space are equally important. Meeting both requirements; i.e., the abstraction and connectivity of heritage, and the interactive functionality of design, implies that an installation that is simultaneously a work of art as well as a design.

3.2 Light as artistic design

The use of light within public art and architecture is not unique, especially in its ability to create public realms [10]. In the past, lighting has been an essential, yet ancillary tool to highlight works of art, or make them visible during the night. With the development of media technology however, lighting has taken a more prominent position as a medium in its own right. At the same time, urban lighting design has widened its scope from that of optimizing the existing architectural environment and urban planning, to assigning itself as a platform which allows users to interact with their surroundings. Urban lighting design and public art share a similar functional development: turning a space to a place, and have thus gravitated towards each other and converged [11, 12]. Designers who were once traditionally viewed as optimizers rather than creators have started to form a more pronounced personal identity by shocking people with bold decisions [13]. Artists, on the other hand, who traditionally sought merely to create a bond between a created object and those who viewed it, have now reached out beyond the viewer and into their physical and metaphysical spaces, adding new value to not just their experience, but equally their surroundings and their lives.

3.3 The key - ownership

As touched upon earlier, user-ownership is an important element in urban development, and is therefore a key aspect of the current proposed lighting installation. Pierce, Kostova & Dirk (2001) have proposed three routes to psychological ownership: intimacy, investment and control. In other words, by intimately knowing, investing in, and controlling the target, the latter of which can be both material and immaterial, one can create psychological ownership.

In addition, in a study on water supply systems, Marks & Davis, (2012) showed that households which contributed to the water projects, rather than pay for them, tended to have a stronger sense of ownership not only over the project, but equally over the materials they frequently used, e.g. pipes, etc.

3.4 The link – ownership in art, design and urban planning

Art and design each relate to different aspects of cognition. The combination of both means that the functionality of design can convey the abstraction of art in the sense of Cupchik & László. Yet besides these general qualities, art and design equally have a more intimate connection with the aspect of ownership, and as a platform can affect urban development. Guetzkow (2002) has argued that art impacts not only mechanisms of the psychological individual, but equally wider cultural and socio-economic mechanisms of the community. As such, art is shown to induce positive psychological responses and boost self-esteem, which are key conditions of ownership. Similar to research on psychological ownership, design-oriented studies equally show the correlation between design and affective response, as well as design and attachment [6].

Ownership has equally been the subject of studies in urban development. Riger & Lavrakas emphasized that by providing opportunities for social interaction, neighbourhoods can provide a sense of belonging for people and thus may foster a "psychological sense of community". Furthermore, it has also been argued that public art should be able to generate a sense of ownership by forging the connection between citizens, city spaces and their meaning as places [14].

3.5 VR as a platform for architectural projects

VR offers users spatial experiences with time and lighting, and the importance of using VR as a presentation tool in architectural fields is well documented. Further, its cost efficiency compared to real construction and maintenance have equally increased demands for VR in various other fields. This is equally relevant in the field of lighting, which is a multidimensional design element, and which is spatial and temporal in nature. Because lighting requires a deeper spatial understanding, researchers are encouraged to use VR as a design tool [15].

4 Design research methodology

The design occurred in two phases: firstly, the area of urban development was analysed to understand the meaning it had for the local inhabitants and users. This was key in identifying the aspects over which ownership would be given during the development of the area. Secondly, the analysis had to be translated into an installation within a lighting art-design framework. This installation would be a platform of interactivity and communication between the local inhabitants and users of the area under development.

Since research on ownership, and its correlation with art and design include disparate research fields, e.g. psychology, urban planning based on site research, and art and design, a tool is needed to weave them together. Because this study deals with social phenomena, an ethnographic approach has been applied to interrelate various factors such as space, actors, feelings, and goals [16]. In this study descriptive observations on the activity area paralleled with focus group interviews for both the quantitative and qualitative data about the users. With respects to the site and the physical environment, the descriptive observation is supported by the TI3 report [17], the formal study for the city plan, and statistical data from Lund Kommune.

The observation and analysis of the individual locations of local activity, i.e., a local farming area and a willow hut area, was conducted based on a descriptive question matrix approach. As such, relevant questions were chosen from the matrix in order to get a better understanding of the meaning and use of the areas [16].

In the analysis of the area, a mixed method approach was applied in which qualitative data and quantitative data were integrated. Each data strand was obtained and analysed separately, and used to enrich the understanding of the data in a holistic sense. As such, the convergent parallel model of mixed method was used [18]. Within this the semi-structured focus group, interviews and observations resulted in qualitative data, whereas the statistical data was quantitative.

4.1 Field research

4.1.1 Activity – analysis and results

The project area was divided into three topological types; research centres, local activity spots, and farming areas (Fig 1). There were three field trips at the beginning of the research, each with a different focus: local activities, topology, and lighting conditions. By observing the area, two spots were determined to be central activities in the area based on size and scope.

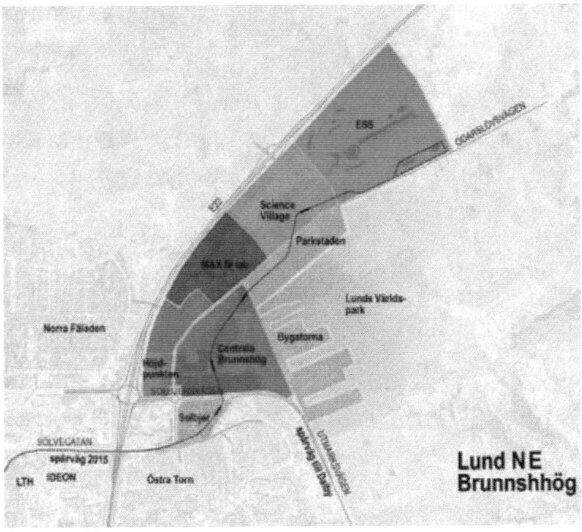

Fig. 1. Project area

Firstly, there is a local cultivation area for growing vegetables, flowers and fruits called Odla i Lund. This area is owned by the commune and offers access for a small fee [19]. It is located in the central part of Brunnshög and has an area of about 2000m2. To date, approximately 600 people have participated in the small-scale farming projects on a regular basis. The community of Odla i Lund have an online website and organize various activities and guest speakers on the topic of agriculture and horticulture.

Secondly, there is an area of fairly dense forest where willow huts are built by local children. It is a cultural and educational spot where local families, including young children, participate in educational activities, and has a more eventful character. Families bring their children to this spot to let them experience nature in a hands-on fashion.

Although the groups who used each area were different, they all revolved around spare time activities where families interact with nature. The local farming area saw mostly adults engaging in small scale agriculture. Children sometimes accompanied their adult family members, i.e., parents or grandparents, to learn about growing vegetables, plants, etc. The focus of activity was different for the willow hut area, where families with children would go exclusively for the children's sake. The activities in the willow hut area focused mainly on building in nature, and experiencing raw, uncultivated nature. In both areas, the presence of nature and the closeness to the earth functions as an essential part of the children's upbringing, and the adults′ well-being. Both activities are actively organized and maintained by the local community of Brunnshög, and include a website. In addition, they receive municipal support, and are promoted as a model for sustainable living.

4.1.2 Topology - analysis and results

Whereas the fieldwork focused on the presence and activity of the groups in the area, the second visit analysed the topology of the site. During this visit, various paths were analysed, including the areas these connected. It was observed that there were more paths and connections to the residential town Norra Fäladen than connections to the large farming areas on the right side of Brunnshög. Further Ideon, a science park which is situated the closest to Solbjer, was directly linked to Brunnshög and within walking distance.

The public transport connection between Lund and Brunsshög, which currently is a bus, passes by Ideon. The municipality however has announced the development of a tram connection to strengthen the connection not only between spots in Brunnshög, but also between Brunnshög and Central Lund.

4.2 Statistics: demographic analysis and results

The Lund Kommune conducted and reported a pilot study called TI3 in 2012 to assess the feasibility of the city plan. It advocated creating a city where scientists and farmers could integrate and create synergy [17]. A more in-depth research into the area was conducted on the basis of statistical data of the municipality relating to other demographics. The demographic data has shown that Lund is a city centred around its university, its cooperative research centres and companies, the latter of which have developed a strong IT infrastructure. The average age in Lund is significantly lower than that of Skåne and the rest of Sweden, with 41% in the 20 to 44 age range [20]. In addition, the largest occupation of this age group was in the IT sector, predominately in mobile and computer technology fields.

4.3 Focus group interview

4.3.1 Target group

The target groups were designed after analysing the data from the field research and formal studies. Three groups were determined based on their integration into the area and their level of IT aptitude. The participants were purposefully chosen to represent the target groups. Three groups were classified: the residents of Brunsshög, young IT professionals from Lund and Malmö, and the young professionals' families. The focus group interview was conducted to firstly map the target groups´ feelings, rhythms and routines, and secondly to determine what they thought was most important to their lives [21].

Due to issues of confidentiality, it was decided to conduct the focus group interview only with employees from Kraftringen, the project owner. Although their background as employees of an energy company were grounds for bias concerns, they were still considered as representative of the target group of IT professionals. A second possible bias was the lack of participants from the two local active communities, i.e., the local small-scale farming club and the willow hut building community. However, those two activity hubs have built their own social networking media such as web pages and YouTube accounts, and had been researched by the municipality before. This data substituted for the lack of representatives from these two communities.

There were 6 participants in total between the ages of 22 and 60 years old. Two participants were in their twenties, two participants were in their forties, and the final two participants were forty and sixty (Fig 2). There were two males and four females (Fig 3). All participants had lived in the greater Lund area (Fig 4) for one to 57 years. One participant who has lived in Malmö for a year had grown up in Lund, and thus it was assumed that all participants had deep connections with the area.

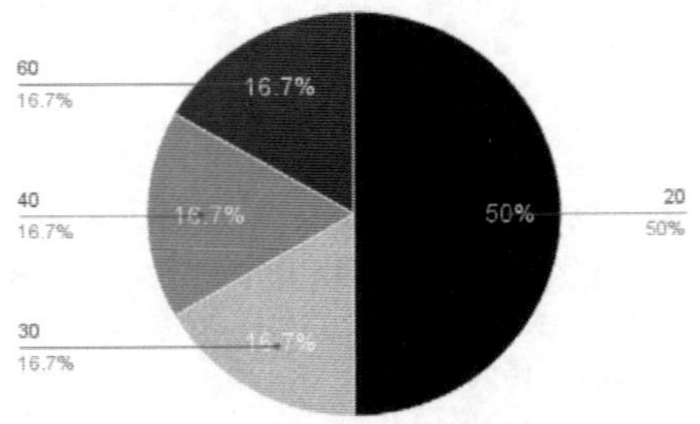

Fig. 2. Age

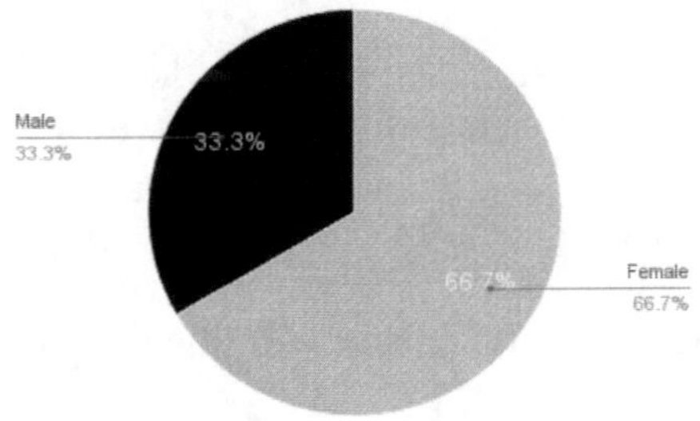

Fig. 3. Gender

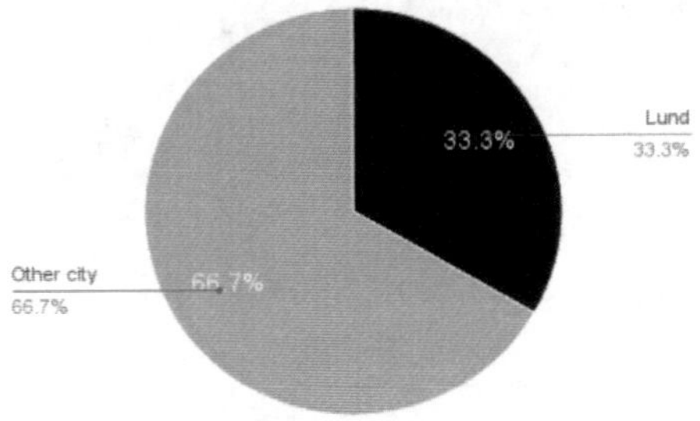

Fig. 4. Living area

4.3.2 Interview methodology

Although focus group interviews are usually conducted along a structured interview methodology, the questions asked in this survey were unstructured, and produced data based on drawings and a review of the discussion. This method was carefully chosen as a tool to capture the ′ineffable sides in their life′, and ′aspects that are not easily stated′ [22]. To avoid bias, the aim of the survey was not revealed to the participants [23].

The interview consisted of a 15-minute drawing session and 15-20-minute discussion session, followed by questions about gender, age, place of residence, and how long they had lived in the area.

As researchers in the area of arts-based methodologies highlight, meaning-making through the arts is full of complexity. The artistic products are themselves texts to be read and interpreted by their producer and their audiences, including researchers. At the same time, the use of drawing as a research method typically involves more than just engaging participants in making drawings, followed by the researcher’s analysis of these artefacts. When drawing is used as a research method, it often entails participants’ drawing and talking or drawing and writing [24].

Easy and normal materials, such as colour pencils and pens, were prepared. It was key that the participants felt comfortable drawing, and were not burdened by feelings of shame for not being capable of producing nice drawings. To reassure them, it was noted that the focus was on the content of their drawing, and not its quality [24].

4.3.3 Interview questions

In the drawing session participants were asked to draw their ideas about three questions: how would you like to play in / with the installation spot, how do you experience electricity, and how do you experience other people. After that they were asked to explain their drawings, discuss it, and share the ideas in a comfortable atmosphere. The questions aimed to understand which conditions can lead to a sense of ownership [Q1] (Fig 5), ideas about technology [Q2] (Fig 6), and their relationship with the people and communities [Q3] (Fig 7).

Questionnaire

Q1: How would you like to play in / with this area? (5 min)
Please draw your idea based on the dimensions with
whom/ when/ how/ how long/ why?

Q2: How do you experience electricity? (5 min)
Q3: How do you experience other people? (5 min)

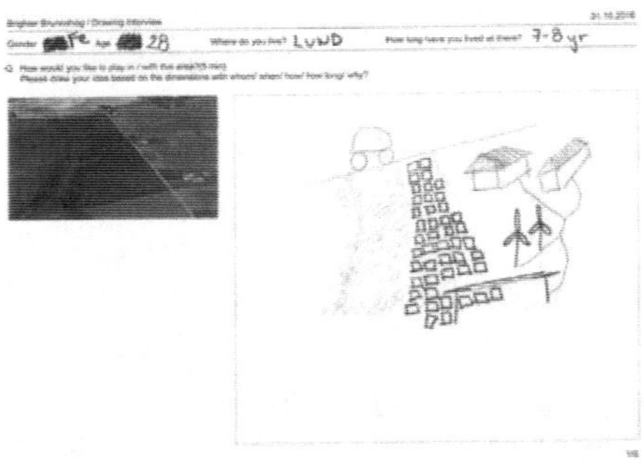

Fig. 5. How would you like to play in / with the area?

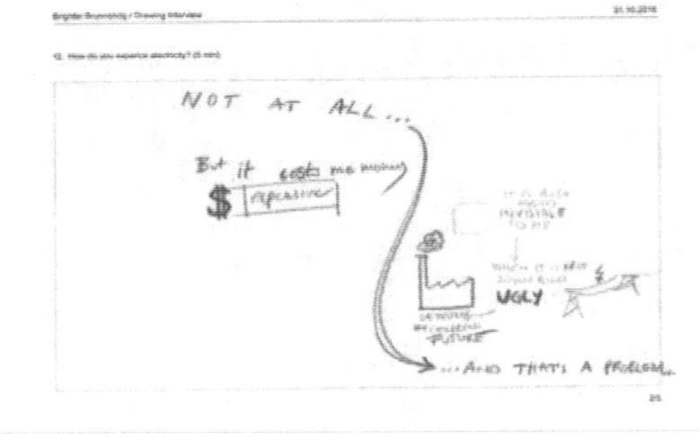

Fig. 6. How do you experience electricity?

Fig. 7. How do you experience other people?

4.3.4 Interview analysis

The discussions after the drawing session were transcribed as the discussion took place. The collected data was analysed by the program N-vivo to clarify the frequency of the keywords, which were subsequently grouped into themes. Most reactions related to the convenience of electricity, i.e,. a better quality of life and better connection between people. This was mentioned 17 times (9.06%) in total during the discussion and was observed as the most frequent. The second most frequently mentioned theme related to the experience of other people, and is described as positive feelings, i.e., cosiness, warm colour lighting therapy, a number of people, soft, calm, nice view. This theme was mentioned 13 times (9,14%). Energy efficiency, related to question two, included the topic of solar panels, electric cars and bicycles, and recycling, and was mentioned 10 times, (4,17%). Outdoor activities, related to question one, included horse riding, walking, running and fishing, and was mentioned nine times (4,20%). Finally, New technology, related to question two, included the topic of new mobile phone applications, GPS, Mega Tetris, Interactive lighting, and Tesla, and was mentioned seven times (3.36%).

There were other trends beyond the five most frequent topics which mostly related to a concern for the environment. The participants recycled daily disposals and reduced energy consumption by being energy efficient, e.g., by using electric cars.

Furthermore, it could be said that they were regularly doing outdoor activities such as jogging, riding, swimming etc. It was suggested that those activities could be an element which could attract people to the installation on a regular basis.

The data indicated that the participants were highly interested in energy efficiency, a bias expected from this group as employees of an energy company.

5 Artistic design development

5.1 Location

The analysis was conducted to determine the main location for the lighting installation, and was based on the design criteria that the installation act as a conduit between the science part of the area with the local communal activity spots. As such, a suitable spot was found in the middle of these two areas with a long open area surrounded by trees running adjacent to the large farm (Fig 8, spot A). Accessibility for both the local and near-town people was a priority, and therefore, the proximity of the chosen spot to public transport and roads was a major determining factor in the choice.

Fig. 8. Project area

The location for the lighting installation is approximately 100 meters from the MAX IV facility, and equally about 100 meters from the small-scale farming area and the adjacent willow huts forest area. There is a road running along the length of the area at about 50 meters, which connects to the road and bus route of the MAX IV facility and the science park, which in turn connects to Lund.

5.2 Theme

The theme for the installation is based on the focus of the development of the area, and the activities of the local users. The urban development is heavily centred on the scientific community, which stands in stark contrast to the local farming and forest activities of the current users. It was felt that ownership over such a conceptual clash in the area could best be given by highlighting the link between technology and raw nature, and how users of nature form the vital link to scientific development. In other words, the local users could feel empowerment and ownership once they realised how the development of science, and as such the area, was dependent on them.

5.3 Design Criteria

On the basis of the requirements of the developers of the area, Kraftringen, and the analysis of the results of the focus group interviews, as well as the chosen theme for the installation project, three criteria were determined as guidelines for the development of the design: awareness, mutuality and adaptability (Fig 9).

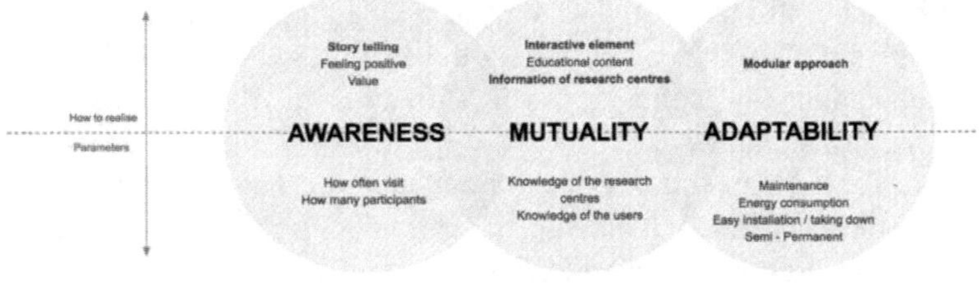

Fig. 9. Three design criteria

Firstly, 'awareness' is proposed to create a feeling of ownership in the development of the area and refers to the user's position as a medium between nature and technology. It was based on the research mostly about the local activities and question one of the focus group interview. It emphasized that the users could be seen as a medium between nature and cutting-edge technologies, i.e., the research centres.

This sense of ownership would be further strengthened by the interactive nature of the installation, the latter of which would make the users feel they are being listened to, and have a say over the development of the area. This is equally the link to the second criterion of 'mutuality', which contains information of users and research centres, so both sides can learn from each other. It is based on the understanding from demographic data that the local- and future users of the area will be tech-savvy and IT professionals, as indicated in the second question of the focus group interviews.

The interactive platform was designed to promote and allow people to easily gain access to the installation spot, and would offer a communication channel between the users and the planners, and policy makers.

Thirdly, 'adaptability' is a requirement from the developers of the area, which will allow the design to follow the stages of area development. This criterion relates to both the functional design of the installation, so it can grow and move as the urban development progresses, as well as the artistic expression of the idea of sustainability, the latter of which was revealed to be important in the focus group interview. As such, it will be easily foldable and movable, and will rely on solar power to run the lights of the installation. Adaptability was achieved by a modular design, which could be expanded upon, or reduced by the use of modules and units. Therefore, a Miura origami tessellation structure was proposed for the adaptable design which users could easily adjust in size and shape through physical interaction.

6 Design proposal

The design itself was decided to represent a portal connecting the undeveloped natural area with the developed area, and was based on the criteria of awareness, mutuality and adaptability. The model was intended to add to the variety of attractions for the chosen spot and to encourage visitors to interact with the objects.

Even though the installation will be in a virtual environment, and outside the effects of gravity, physics and weather conditions, the design still carefully considered the condition of the physical place to create a believable environment.

6.1 Tessellation structure

The basic module is a Miura-ori Tessellation structure (Fig 10). It is easy to stretch and fold, and can be extended by combining several modules.

Its high flexibility, i.e., foldability, was used to give a greater sense of interaction. Further, the structure is represented as stable to create a believable sense for the users who know the windy weather conditions of Brunnshög, yet with the ability to create a dramatic effect through its transforming capability.

The tessellation tunnel can thus be used by users to create a physical area which will invite people, and make them walk inside and through it. The ability to expand and compress the tunnel equally gives a greater sense of control over the object.

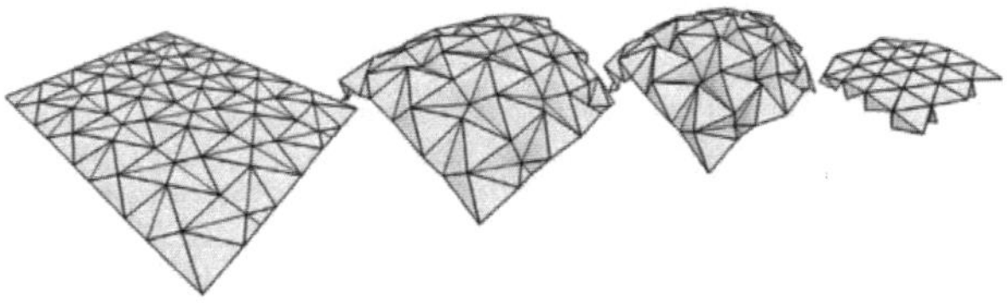

Fig. 10. An example of a Miura-ori tessellation structure.

Fig. 11. Tessellation tunnel

Fig. 12. Tessellation tunnel in VR

The default figure of the tunnel is short and more spherical, which when expanded, assumes a longer and semi-circular shape (Fig. 11). This creates a tunnel which faces both sides: the activity area and the research centres. At the same time the tunnel in and of itself will signify a gate of its own, connecting nature, i.e., the activity areas, with the technology areas. As such, it should stimulate a sense of awareness for the users as a medium between raw nature and cutting-edge technology. The tunnel was created using Blender and rendered in real time in Unreal Engine 4 (UE4) and transferred to its virtual environment (Fig. 12).

The structure acts as the platform for lighting delivery, and is based on three types of interactivity. Firstly, the users can manipulate the colours and intensity of the light of the tunnel by using the sensors in HTC Vive controllers. Secondly, the users' physical activity, i.e., touching the LED panels on the surfaces inside of the tunnel, changes the lighting patterns on the panels. These two main interactions can create the participants' own lighting design inside the tunnel. To change the patterns of the panel, the users are required to reach the panel. This means they have to jump or run to light up the panels in certain locations. This interaction design was proposed to encourage the users' physical movement as they are familiar with outdoor activities such as gardening, building, and horse riding. Finally, the shape of the installation is also interactive. In this interactive layer the transforming object indicates the presence of users, and it welcomes the users by opening up when it detects their presence.

By applying the same interactive concept and content to the tunnel, the users are encouraged to feel that they are participating and involved in the development project, which can stimulate the sense of ownership over the area and the development.

6.2 Virtual environments – interaction and awareness

The virtual environment was created in UE4 with various 2D, 3D programs such as Rhino, Blender and Photoshop. The size of the area was approximately 600x600m and based on the topological data from Google Earth, as well as field research, since the virtual environment primarily aimed to mimic the nature in Brunnshög in as much detail as possible (Fig. 13). The tunnel was situated in the middle of the project area as a portal and connection between the new research centres and the farming area. The users were encouraged to walk through the tunnel and interact with it by changing the LED light panels (Fig. 14).

Fig. 13. Level design

Fig. 14. Simulated LED panel

The lighting patterns in the LED panel were inspired by the neutron spallation system of the two research centres; MAX IV and ESS. They are both spallation research facilities based on different systems; MAX IV uses a circular system, and ESS (European Spallation Source) uses a linear one. The lighting patterns are designed to represent these circular and linear movements to help the users to understand the research facilities in a fun way (Fig.15).

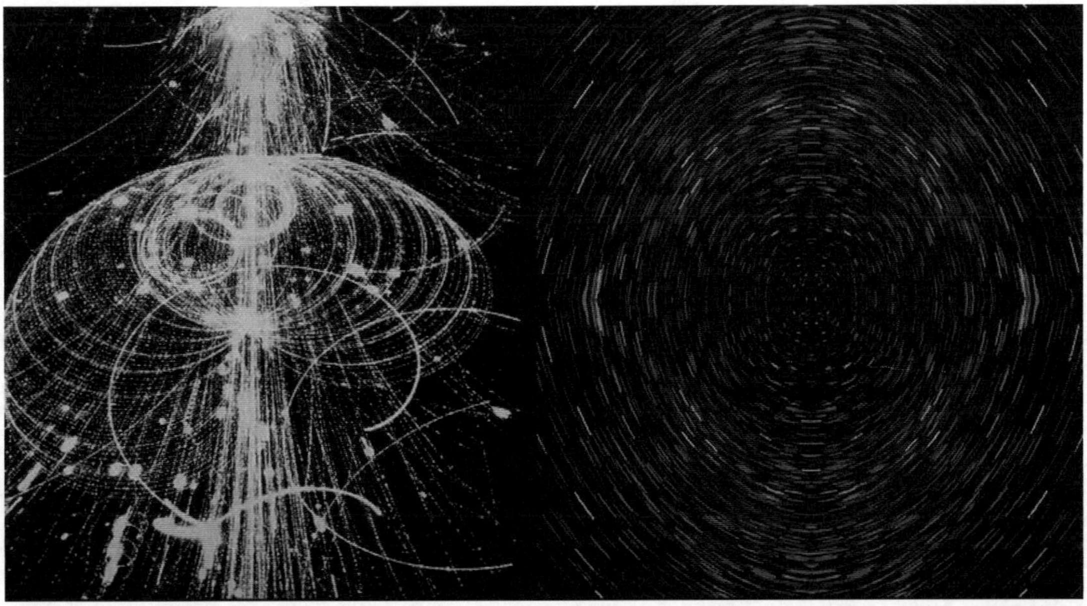

Fig. 15. Lighting patterns inspired from the spallation systems

The tunnel invites the users to pass through, and represents a journey from the undeveloped natural area to the developed area. Along the direction of the tunnel, users interact with the tunnel, which primes them to understand the development of the new area. When the users exit the tunnel, they can visit several buildings that have already been built as part of the development project, and get information about these new research centres. Several landmarks in Brunnshög and Lund were equally created to inform the users with topological information of the area. By encouraging the users to navigate the areas to collect the information, the users can understand more about the past, present, and future of Brunnshög. With this better knowledge of the area, the users are encouraged to feel that they really know the area, the latter of which is a fundamental condition to create a sense of ownership over the area.

7 Test

The proposed design has shown that an art-based lighting design is feasible to create art, and combine it with design based on research, and that in line with any research, it can be tested with respects to falsifiability to see if, in this case, the installation provides a sense of ownership over the urban development project [25].

The test for the hypothesis was conducted by qualitatively assessing parameters connected to notions of a ′sense of ownership′. These parameters were studied before and after the participants experienced the installation and the virtual environment.

7.1 Pilot test

An early pilot study on 21 subjects, ages25 to 59, was conducted to assess the feasibility and the design of the tests. The test subjects who participated in the pilot study were employees from Kraftringen, the project owner.

Overall, the test clearly showed that the experience of the lighting art installation in virtual reality increased the awareness of the area and a positive attitude toward the development of the area. The test questions were formulated to firstly ask the about users' perception, knowledge, and the connections to the area before and after their experience of VR. Secondly, the users were asked if they felt a sense of control and participation during their experience in the tunnel. (Fig. 16). In the first part of the questions, the users answered that they had more positive feelings of Brunnshög, and more knowledge of the development of the area. They also felt the development connected to sustainability, innovation and technology. Nevertheless, their feeling of control and participation in the interaction of the tunnel was not strong, and it was considered that this was primarily due to the complexity of interaction with controllers. Furthermore, this pilot study equally indicated that it was difficult to detect signs and paths while the users navigated the area. (Table.1). Therefore, after careful consideration and research about perception of visual recognition and optimized UX design, the level design was optimized by applying emissive materials on signs and removing some foliage on the path in the virtual Brunnshög. Furthermore, the lighting interaction was simplified by using only one controller. (Fig.17).

The results were considered biased since the employees of the project owner had a greater chance of being exposed to information about the project.

Questionnaire:

1. How do you feel about the current Brunnshög? (Scale 1-5)
   Nothing special | 1 | 2 | 3 | 4 | 5 | Very positive
2. To what extent do you feel that you have knowledge about the development and future of Brunnshög? ? (Scale 1-5)
   Not at all | 1 | 2 | 3 | 4 | 5 | Very much
3. To what extent do you feel curious about the development and future of Brunnshög? (Scale 1-5)
   Not at all | 1 | 2 | 3 | 4 | 5 | Very much
4. To what extent do you connect the future – developed – Brunnshög with sustainability? (Scale 1-5)
   Not at all | 1 | 2 | 3 | 4 | 5 | Very much
5. To what extent do you connect the future – developed – Brunnshög with innovation? (Scale 1-5)
   Not at all | 1 | 2 | 3 | 4 | 5 | Very much
6. To what extent do you connect the future – developed – Brunnshög with new technology? (Scale 1-5)
   Not at all | 1 | 2 | 3 | 4 | 5 | Very much
7. To what extent do you feel that you have a connection to Brunnshög? (Scale 1-5)
   No connection at all | 1 | 2 | 3 | 4 | 5 | Very much
8. To what extent would you like to visit Brunnshög in your leisure time? (Scale 1-5)
   Not at all | 1 | 2 | 3 | 4 | 5 | Very much
9. To what extent do you feel you have control over the lighting patterns in the tunnel? (Scale 1-5)
   No control at all | 1 | 2 | 3 | 4 | 5 | Total control
10. How did you create the lighting patterns in the tunnel? (Scale 1-5)
   I was playing around | 1 | 2 | 3 | 4 | 5 | I made an effort to create something
11. Do you feel like you are part of something bigger when you create lighting patterns in the tunnel? (Scale 1-5)
   Not at all | 1 | 2 | 3 | 4 | 5 | Very much
12. Do you feel the VR experience gives you knowledge about the future of Brunnshög? (Scale 1-5)
   Not at all | 1 | 2 | 3 | 4 | 5 | Very much
13. Room for comments:

Fig. 16. Questionnaire for pilot test

Table 1. Data from the pilot test

	Question nbr (before):								Question nbr (after):																
Participan	Q1	Q2	Q3	Q4	Q5	Q6	Q7	Q8	Q1	Q2	Q3	Q4	Q5	Q6	Q7	Q8	Q9	Q10	Q11	Q12	Gender (Male/ Female)	Age	Visual impairment that affects the VR-experience?	Resident in Lund?	Ever Been to Brunnshög?
1	1	3	5	4	4	4	2	4	1	3	5	4	4	4	3	5	3	2	2	2	M	32	N	N	Rarely
2	3	2	4	4	4	3	1	2	2	3	4	4	4	4	2	2	3	3	3	3	M	43	N	N	Yearly
3	3	2	4	4	4	4	1	2	3	4	4	5	5	5	3	4	4	2	3	4	F	27	N	Y	Rarely
4	5	3	5	4	5	5	3	5	5	4	5	4	5	5	4	5	x	x	x	x	M	48	N	N	Rarely
5	3	3	5	5	5	5	4	5	5	3	6	6	5	5	4	5	3	5	5	5	M	56	C	N	No
6	5	5	5	5	4	4	5	3	5	5	5	5	4	4	5	4	4	3	4	5	M	59	N	N	Monthly
7	4	4	4	3	4	5	4	3	4	4	4	4	5	5	4	4	4	2	3	2	M	38	C	Y	Yearly
8	3	4	3	3	3	4	2	2	3	4	3	3	3	3	2	2	2	1	1	1	M	54	C	Y	Monthly
9	1	2	5	4	5	5	1	4	4	3	5	4	5	5	3	5	4	1	4	5	F	38	N	Y	Yearly
10	1	3	3	2	4	4	1	3	2	2	3	3	3	3	1	3	2	1	1	2	M	28	N	N	Rarely
11	4	2	3	3	3	3	2	2	4	3	4	4	4	4	3	3	4	2	3	4	M	37	N	N	No
12	2	4	5	4	3	3	3	5	4	4	5	4	4	3	3	5	2	2	2	3	M	51	C	N	Yearly
13	3	3	4	4	4	4	2	3	5	4	5	5	5	5	5	4	5	1	3	4	M	28	N	Y	Rarely
14	5	3	5	5	4	4	4	3	5	4	5	5	4	4	4	4	4	1	4	4	F	54	P	Y	Yearly
15	1	2	4	5	5	5	3	1	2	2	5	5	5	5	4	4	4	2	3	4	F	50	B,P	N	Yearly
16	1	4	5	5	5	4	2	1	1	4	5	5	5	5	3	1	4	1	3	4	M	26	N	Y	Yearly
17	4	4	4	5	5	4	3	3	3	4	5	4	5	5	4	4	3	1	3	3	F	25	N	N	Yearly
18	5	5	5	5	5	5	5	4	5	5	5	5	5	5	5	5	3	1	3	3	M	28	N	Y	Yearly
19	4	5	4	4	5	5	4	2	4	5	4	4	5	5	4	2	2	1	2	1	M	52	N	Y	Monthly
	58	63	82	78	81	80	52	57	67	70	87	83	85	84	66	71	60	32	52	59					
Average	3.05	3.32	4.32	4.11	4.26	4.21	2.74	3.00	3.53	3.68	4.58	4.37	4.47	4.42	3.47	3.74	3.33	1.78	2.89	3.28					
Percent	*16%*	*11%*	*6%*	*6%*	*5%*	*5%*	*27%*	*25%*																	
Percentag	**9%**	**7%**	**5%**	**5%**	**4%**	**4%**	**15%**	**15%**																	
																							C- Corrected P-presbyopia B - Color blind		

Fig. 17. Controller

7.2 Test

The test was conducted on 16th of Sep in IKDC, Lund, Sweden, where the project was presented during Kulturenatten 2017 in Lund, Sweden. As the city hosts many international residents belonging to the university and global companies, the tests were prepared in Swedish and English.

7.2.1 Participants

In total, 22 subjects volunteered to participate. Before they tried the VR simulation, each was asked to complete a questionnaire regarding gender, vision, age, living of area and if they had knowledge of Brunnshög. After completing the form, each participant was escorted into the VR room. The participants were tested separately, which took around 5 minutes each, and afterwards they were asked again to fill in the questionnaire. The two questionnaires were the same in order to assess whether, and in which way, the VR experience could change the participant's opinions.

The ages of the participants were between 12 and 50 years, with 6 participants who did not fill in their age. The mean was 35.6 years, the median was 37 years, and the standard deviation was 10.85. Of the 22 participants, 7 were women (31.8%), 9 were men (40.1%), and 6 did not mention their gender (27%). 11 of the participants (50%, 4 males, 4 females, 3 unknown gender) reported normal vision. 8 participants (36.3%, 4 males, 3 females, 1 unknown gender) stated that they required, and were wearing glasses. Two participants with unknown gender did not report the condition of their vision, and only one participant (4.5%, male) was colour blind. 16 participants (72.7%, 10 males, 6 females) reported they were residents in Lund, and two participants (9%, unknown gender) did not state where they lived. Four participants (18.1%, 1 male, 2 females, 1 unknown gender) answered they visited Brunnshög less than once in a year, four participants (18.1%, 1 male, 1 female, 2 unknown gender) stated they visited Brunnshög annually, three participants (13.6%, 2 males, 1 female) stated that they visited the area on a monthly basis, three participants (13.6%. 1 male, 2 unknown gender) stated that they dropped by the area on a daily basis, five participants (22.7%, 2 males, 3 females) said they had never visited Brunnshög, and two participants with unknown gender did not state whether or not they visited Brunnshög (Table 2).

7.2.2 Test methodology

The questionnaire was conducted in front of the VR room, which was 4x4m2 and which had its windows and walls covered with a dark green fabric. The questionnaire was optimized based on the results of the pilot test. The questionnaire used a 5-step Likert scale, and had an open comment box. The questions were divided into three sections. The first section asked about the participants' demographic information such as age, gender and living area. In the second section, the participants were asked about their attitude and knowledge of the development of the area. These two sections were answered by the participants before and after their experience in the VR installation. An additional section was added in the questionnaire after the VR experience, which related to the topic of control and experience. Within this, the users were asked if they felt sense of control over the lighting patterns, and if the interaction gave them a sense of being involved in something greater. (Table 2). Two instructors guided the test outside of the VR room. Further, participants were instructed in the use of the controller while they waited for their turn. Due to time constraints, and based on the pilot test, the time for the experience for each person was set to 5 min.

7.3 Findings and analysis

7.3.1 Attitude and awareness

The VR experience influenced the users' attitude and awareness about the area. The participants had generally neutral feelings toward the Brunnshög area. After the experience there was a 13 % increase in positive attitude.

In the category of awareness, there was an increase in the following sub-categories: knowledge and curiosity about the project, knowledge about the connection of the project to sustainability, and innovation and new technology.

Knowledge and curiosity about the development of Brunnshög increased by 15% and 16% respectively after experiencing the VR installation. In the sub-categories relating to knowledge about the project and sustainability, innovation and new technology, there was equally an increase in awareness. Prior to the VR experience, users had already connected the future development of Brunnshög to sustainability, yet this increased by 17 percent after the VR experience. This was equally the case for the project´s connection to the idea of innovation and new technology. Although there were already a few users who had some awareness that the development project had something to do with innovation and new technology, after the VR-experience, this increased by 16% and 11% percent respectively. In addition, the users' sense of connection to the area was initially low, yet increased by 15% after the VR experience. Finally, although few indicated they would visit the area in their leisure time, the desire to visit was increased by 13% after the VR experience.

7.3.2 Feeling of control and involvedness in the development

As opposed to the categories of attitude and awareness of the development of the area, assessing the sense of control and importance for the development of the area was more complicated with a greater variety of responses. Regarding the sense of control over the lighting patterns, 13 participants (59%, 7 males, 5 females, one unknown gender) reported that they had a great sense of control (Likert scale 4), but one participant (4.5%, female) reported she did not have control. Overall however, the participants stated that they felt they had control over the lighting patterns (73% positive). They felt that they played with the light rather than creating something special (48% positive). Four participants (18.1%, 2 males, 2 females) reported they felt they created something special, whereas seven participants (31.8% 4 males, 2 females, 1 unknown gender) said they just played with the light. The participant's sense of being part of something bigger were also very contradictory. While nine participants (41%, 3 males, 4 females, 2 unknown gender) reported they felt they were part of something bigger (Likert scale 4), ten participants (45%, 5 males, 1 female, 4 unknown gender) marked lower than a 2 on the Likert scale (57% positive).

Table 2. Data from the test

16/09/2017	Question nbr (before):								Question nbr (after):												General information				
Visitor nbr	Q1	Q2	Q3	Q4	Q5	Q6	Q7	Q8	Q1	Q2	Q3	Q4	Q5	Q6	Q7	Q8	Q9	Q10	Q11	Q12	Gender	Age	Visual imparim ent that affects the VR-experien ce?	Resident in Lund?	Ever Been to Brunnshög?
1	3	1	1	5	5	5	1	3	5	5	5	5	5	5	5	3	5	5	5	5	F	25	N	Y	< 1 time/yr
2	1	2	2	2	2	1	1	1	1	3	3	4	4	4	2	2	5	5	4	3	M	37	N	Y	< 1 time/yr
3	3	5	5	5	5	5	3	5	5	5	5	5	5	5	5	5	5	5	5	5	F	50	N	N	No
4	5	3	4	3	5	5	2	3	4	4	5	3	5	5	3	3	4	2	2	4	M	43	N	N	Monthly
5	2	2	4	4	4	5	3	3	5	4	5	5	5	4	5	4	4	1	3	4	F	28	C	Y	Nej
6	4	2	4	2	3	2	2	3	4	3	5	5	5	4	2	3	1	2	2	3	F	40	N	Y	Nej
7	4	3	4	2	5	4	3	3	4	4	4	3	5	5	3	4	4	5	2	3	M	49	C	Y	Yearly
8	4	3	4	5	5	5	4	4	5	4	5	5	5	5	5	5	4	2	4	5	F	49	C	Y	Yearly
9	3	3	4	4	4	5	4	3	5	4	5	5	5	5	5	5	5	3	4	4	M	45	C	Y	Monthly
10	1	1	5	1	1	3	1	3	1	2	5	2	5	5	2	3	3	1	1	3	-	-	-	-	-
11	1	3	3	4	5	5	1	3	3	3	4	5	5	5	2	4	3	2	2	3	M	20	C	Y	No
12	1	2	2	1	5	5	1	2	2	1	3	1	5	5	2	4	3	1	1	2	M	24	C	Y	-
13	2	2	3	2	3	2	2	1	2	3	3	3	3	3	2	2	2	1	1	2	-	-	C	Y	Yearly
14	1	2	3	4	4	5	1	1	1	2	3	4	5	5	1	2	3	1	3	3	F	26	N	Y	< 1 time/yr
15	1	1	1	1	1		1	1	3	3	5	5	5		1	1	5	1	1	5	M	12	N	N	No
16	3	3	3	3	4	4	3	4	4	3	4	3	4	5	3	4	4	3	5	4	-	-	N	Y	Yearly
17	3	4	5	3	4	4	2	4	3	3	5	4	4	4	4	4	4	4	4	4	F	49	C	Y	Monthly
18	5	4	5	3	5	5	3	4	5	4	4	3	5	5	4	4	2	2	1	2	-	-	-	-	-
19	4	3	3	4	3	4	2	2	3	4	4	4	4	4	3	3	2	2	4	4	-	-	C	Y	Daily
20	2	4	4	5	5	5	3	2	2	4	5	5	5	5	3	3	4	2	3	3	Man	44	B	Y	Daily
21	3	2	3	3	3	2	2	3	4	4	4	5	5	4	3	4	3	2	2	3	-	-	N	Y	< 1 time/yr
22	2	3	5	3	4	4	5	1	1	2	4	4	4	5	2	1	5	1	4	4	Man	29	N	N	Daily
	58	58	77	69	85	85	50	59	72	74	95	88	103	97	67	73	80	53	63	78					
Average grade	2.6	2.6	3.5	3.1	3.9	3.9	2.3	2.7	3.3	3.4	4.3	4.0	4.7	4.4	3.0	3.3	3.6	2.4	2.9	3.5					
Median grade	3.0	3.0	4.0	3.0	4.0	5.0	2.0	3.0	3.5	3.5	4.5	4.0	5.0	5.0	3.0	3.5	4.0	2.0	3.0	3.5					
Increase (in percentage)	13%	15%	16%	17%	16%	11%	15%	13%									73%	48%	57%	71%					

8 Discussion and conclusion

This article explored the potential of using interactive lighting art installations in virtual environments to stimulate a sense of ownership over the urban development of Brunnshög, Sweden. As psychological ownership is a complex phenomenon which can be achieved under certain conditions, this research tried to weave various relevant elements from the wider scope of art, design, anthropology, psychology and urban development studies in the design development of this project. Thus, the design aimed to create an installation which fostered the users' knowledge, sense of control, and feeling of involvement over the area which was under development.

It was highlighted during the urban planning for Brunnshog that the current residents of the area had not been integrated in the planning, even though they were a central element of the local identity and culture. As such, the designers set out to integrate the local residents in a design in which the residents became the conduit between the past, present and future of the area, based on three design criteria: awareness, mutuality and adaptability. Awareness was achieved through the virtual visualization of Brunnshög in which information about the future plans were virtually displayed in a 3D immersive environment. Mutuality criterion was carried out by encouraging users to interact with the tunnel installation and allowing them to explore "Virtual Brunnshög". Finally, by requiring an adaptable approach to design, VR technology allowed the exhibit to be demonstrated anywhere with a minimum amount of equipment and time: a computer and HMD. It equally made it easily accessible for people, including those with disabilities.

Regarding the design of the actual lighting installation, the conducted research on the area and its residents, resulted in the proposal of the tessellation tunnel that was meant to symbolize a portal connecting the current and future Brunnshög. Participants were encouraged to interact with light inside the virtual tunnel and create their own lighting design while they walked through and, in the direction of, where the future Brunnshög was displayed. The interaction was designed to allow for a simple control over the lights and patterns inside the installation.

This project was realized in a virtual environment with UE4 and various 2D, 3D programs, and experienced through HTC Vive. It was cost effective compared to constructing and maintaining a real installation in terms of budget and safety. The test results indicated an increase in positive attitude, as well as knowledge of the area and its development after experience of the VR-installation. With respects to the sense of control and sense of involvement, these were shown to increase partially, yet remained inconclusive due to the variation in responses on the whole.

Based on the overall test results of the effects of the lighting art installation in its virtual environment, this paper argues for the use of VR based lighting art installations as a cost-effective platform in multi-disciplinary urban design projects to affect a positive involvement of inhabitants. Although the results remain inconclusive with respects to sense of ownership, there were strong indications that its prerequisites, i.e., knowledge, sense of control and involvedness were positively affected by the experience of the installation, with almost half of the participants stating that they felt they were part of something bigger.

The present study builds upon a previous study [15] by exploring the usage of Virtual Environments in the process of designing and experiencing lighting installations. It was previously explored how VR's ability to create spatial experiences enabled designers to conceptually experiment with their designs digitally [15]. This paper attempted to understand how content and interaction could increase and strengthen the usage of VR technology in lighting design. In particular, it sought to understand how the experience of virtual lighting installations and virtual spaces could achieve familiarity and a sense of ownership over urban development projects.

9 Acknowledgments

This work was held in the context of the project Lighting Metropolis, a collaboration between Kraftringen, Aalborg University Copenhagen and Lund Municipality. The authors would like to especially thank Sara Kralmark , Eva Erdös from Kraftringen, and Andrei-Ducu Predescu from Aalborg University for their great feedback and support.

References

1. L. Scannell, R. Gifford, *Defining Place Attachment: A tripartite organizing framework*, Journal of Environmental Psychology, **30**(1), 1-10 (2010)
2. D. Kahneman, A. Tversky, Choices, Values, and Frames, APA, 39(4), 341-350 (1984)
3. S. Marks, J. Davis, *Does User Participation Lead to Sense of Ownership for Rural Water Systems? Evidence from Kenya*. World Development, **40**(8), 1569-1576 (2012)
4. J. Reb, T. Connolly, *Possession, Feelings of Ownership, and the Endowment Effect*, Judgement and Decision Making, **2**(2), 107-114 (2007)
5. M. Strahilevitz, G. Loewenstein, *The Effect of Ownership History on the Valuation of Objects*, Journal of Consumer Research, **25**(3), 276-289, (1998)

6. W. Baxter, M. Aurisicchio and P. Childs, *A psychological ownership approach to designing object attachment*, Journal of Engineering Design, **26** (4-6), 140-156 (2015)
7. L. Van Dyne, J. Pierce, *Psychological Ownership and Feelings of Possession: three field studies predicting employee attitudes and organizational citizenship behavior*, Journal of Organizational Behavior, **25**(4), 439-459 (2004)
8. D. Vandewalle, L. Van Dyne, T. Kostova, *Psychological Ownership: An Empirical Examination of its Consequences*. Group & Organization Management, **20**(2), 210-226 (1995)
9. G. Cupchik, J. Laszlo, *Emerging Visions of the Aesthetic Process*, Cambridge: Cambridge University Press.1st ed., **53**(4): 64-83. (1992)
10. S, Schemel, F. Dohna, L. Schwendinger, *Cities Alive: Rethinking the Shades of Night*, (Foresight, Arup, 2015)
11. M. Arefi, *Non-place and placelessness as narratives of loss: Rethinking the notion of place*, Journal of Urban Design, vol. **4**, no. 2, 179-193 (1999)
12. E. J. Lee, S.H.Ryu, *A study on the development of the site-specific public art in public design*, KSBDA, **14**(20), 299 (2013)
13. E. Sanders, P. Stappers, *Co-creation and the New Landscapes of Design*, Codesign, **4**(1), 5-18 (2008)
14. J. Sharp, V. Pollock, R. Paddison, *Just Art for a Just City: Public art and social inclusion in urban regeneration*, Urban Studies, **42**(5), 1001-1023 (2005)
15. B. Kim, E. Xylakis, G. Triantafyllidis, *Designing a Lighting Installation through Virtual Reality Technology- the Brighter Brunnshög case study*, ArtsIT 2017, (to be published)
16. N. Tannenbaum, J. Spradley, *Participant Observation*, Anthropological Quarterly, **53**(4), 260 (1980)
17. Lunds Kommun, TI3 (Holmbergs, 2012)
18. J.W. Creswell, V. L. Clark, Designing and Conducting Mixed Methods Research (Sage, 2011)
19. *Stadsodling - Odla i Lund - Uppleva & göra - Lund*, Lund.se. Retrieved 27 December, from https://www.lund.se/odlailund (2016)
20. Lunds Kommun, *Municipal facts* (Scb.se, 2016)
21. J. Billson, *Conducting focus group research across culture*, WeD, 27 (2006)
22. S. Weber, *Visual Image in Research*, in J. G. Knowles & A. L. Cole (Eds.), Handbook of the arts in qualitative research: Perspectives, methodologies, examples, and issues, (Sage, Los Angeles, 2008)
23. D. Morgan, *Focus groups as qualitative research*, Thousand Oaks, Calif, 1, 32-46 (1997)
24. L. Theron, C. Mitchell, A. Smith, J. Stuart, Picturing research (Sense, Rotterdam, 2011)
25. M. Kendall, K. Popper, *The Logic of Scientific Discovery*, Biometrika, **46**(12), 265, (1959)

Filling the gaps: shaping lighting. Education for the future

P. Bech-Larsen[1], *S. Linnebjerg*[1] *and M.F. Mullins*[1]
[1] Aalborg University, Copenhagen, Denmark
pbl@create.aau.dk sl@create.aau.dk mullins@create.aau.dk

Abstract. Training and knowledge of lighting is an increasingly sought-after professional quality in Denmark and Sweden. However, technological development in the lighting field has been in recent years extremely rapid, not least in Scandinavia. This has led to a situation, where users, designers, specifiers, buyers and installers are often neither in possession, nor have access to, the knowledge about lighting that they need. The aim of the study is to map and analyze the existing offer and demand for competencies within lighting related fields. That is to say, the study has looked at the existing educational programs within a broad field of lighting and compared this 'supply' to the current 'demand' by local employers. The paper presents the results from a statistical analysis of data collected from a series of surveys, expert interviews and focus groups, involving more than 250 participants in Sweden and Denmark. Based on the findings, the paper presents recommendations for the design of educational curricula.

1 Introduction

Light has been shown to have a significant impact on our daily lives in such fields as health, learning, work and general wellbeing (Schlangen et al., 2014). Training and knowledge of lighting is therefore becoming a more widely sought professional quality in Denmark and Sweden. However, technological development in the lighting field has in recent years been extremely rapid, not least in Scandinavia. This has led to a situation, where users, designers, specifiers, buyers and installers have in many cases been outpaced and are neither in possession nor have access to the knowledge about lighting that they need. For example, latest LED developments entail completely new prerequisites for electricians, electrical installers, architects, urban planners and municipalities. Another example is that IT educational programs should today include the development of programming skills that are required by 'intelligent' lighting. For the purpose of this study, these bottlenecks are referred to the 'gaps' between the existing educational offer and industry's demand.

The quantifying and mapping of the supply and demand for lighting-related competencies in Denmark and Sweden provides the basis for the investigation of the current gaps. The study has investigated the relation between the demand, driven by the labor market, and the educational offer within the interdisciplinary field of lighting, through a series of extensive surveys that helped collect data on the current situation in Greater Copenhagen.

The aim of the study was to map and analyze the present offer and demand for competencies within lighting related fields. That is to say, the study looked at the existing educational programs within a broad field of lighting and compared this 'supply' to the current 'demand' by local employers.

The research identifies and contributes to the establishment and growth of underdeveloped or lacking competencies in the region. This approach attempts to lay the foundation for a comprehensive strategy for reducing the 'gap' between labor demand and the provision of educational services in the lighting field. Mapping the existing competencies can also strengthen and expand lighting education in the region by opening up new possibilities for collaboration between municipalities, industry and educational institutions. Establishing future scenarios within this context can pave the way for new beneficial partnerships with the aim to improve their international competitiveness. Building a strong relation between educators and employers in the region can be beneficial for all parties, including municipalities, private companies as well as educational institutions themselves. The field of lighting is rapidly developing and expanding to include an increasing number of disciplines varying from technical and humanistic to artistic practices both on a practical and theoretical level. The goal of the study is therefore to provide an overview to support the development of a comprehensive strategy that reflects the labor market demand, together with the design and organization of the supply-side of the lighting education. The purpose is thus to ensure that well-trained lighting professionals graduate from the educational programs that support the interdisciplinary lighting industry in Greater Copenhagen.

2 Method

2.1 Surveys

To define the primary themes for this research project, a broad range of competencies were identified within the field of lighting. To validate these competencies and categories, a focus group with selected participants was presented with an initial definition, and the competencies and categories were developed based on the focus group discussion. The results were compared with the previous findings obtained from LYSNET.dk and the "key topics" identified in the DCL report (Dansk Center for Lys & Innovationsnetværket Dansk Lys, 2012). The final set included 111 competencies and 8 categories. Next, the extensive screening of educational programs in Denmark and Sweden was carried out to identify which programs potentially offer relevant lighting related courses. The analysed educational institutions included universities, university colleges, architectural schools, engineering colleges, stage and art schools, Swedish Högskolar, as well as professional bachelor programs, including those that train electricians.

Relevant search-words were identified and a comprehensive online search was performed for each of the competencies. Based on the findings from UddannelsesGuiden (www.ug.dk), studere.nu and studentum.se, almost 300 educational programs were found to be potentially relevant to the 111 competencies; of these 150 were included in the survey, based on a fine-meshed screening. Online surveys were designed using SurveyXact for all 111 competencies, divided into eight topics. The questions employed a Likert scale to determine the degree to which the included educational programs "supply" the 111 competencies. The questionnaire was tested with 15 selected participants to identify errors. In January 2017, 152 respondents from different educational programs were contacted by phone before the launch of the survey in order to encourage and motivate participation. The selection of this group was based on a spread of the different professionals (within groups such as architecture, engineering, technical etc.); different types of educational programs; and the extent to which the educational institutions were estimated to provide lighting-related competencies. The 'supply' survey was completed and distributed by early

February 2017. All respondents were sent two reminders and 84 valid responses were received. Subsequently, a similar online survey was designed to establish the 'demand' for the 111 competencies by companies and municipalities. Relevant contact persons were identified via industry related websites and Danish and Swedish light associations, such as: Innovationsnetværk Dansk Lys (DK), Elforsk (DK), Lysnet. dk (DK), Sydljus (SE), Ljuskultur (SE), Belysningsbrachen (SE) and Lighting Metropolis (DK + SE). The survey was also advertised in the newsletters for members of DCL (Dansk Center for Lys, DK) and Sydljus (SE). Personal email addresses were gathered online and all demand-participants received the survey by email, with an introduction to the project via SurveyXact. A few random people received a phone call or a personal email. This effort resulted in the database of 435 contact persons and 92 valid answers.

2.2 Analysis

Data obtained from the 'supply' survey were subjected to a descriptive analysis. Subsequently, the data obtained from the 'demand' surveys were also analyzed by descriptive analysis. The results of the two initial survey analyses were then compared and major gaps between the supply and demand of the identified competences were identified. Next, Wilcoxon Signed-Rank statistical tests were carried out on the survey results, where the 'supply' answers were paired with the 'demand' answers. This non-parametric test is suitable for paired samples and is based on the ranks of the absolute difference in the values of each pair of Likert scale responses. The findings of the initial descriptive analysis were generally supported by the statistical methods.

To validate the results of the statistically significant gaps and the future possibilities of research, education and collaboration, we interviewed 17 prominent European experts in lighting. Interviews were partially transcribed, highlighting only relevant parts of the interviews. The quantitative results of the current situation in Denmark and Sweden, combined with the qualitative findings from the expert interviews, resulted in several hypotheses formulated for the current situation, the immediate future and for a 5-10 year perspective.

In June 2017, 14 representatives of industry, municipalities and educational institutions from Denmark and Sweden met at Aalborg University in Copenhagen to take part in two focus groups. The results obtained from the surveys, as well as other findings and the preliminary hypotheses formulated based on the series of expert interviews were presented to the participants of these two focus groups. The final analysis was carried out to review the new information, reflect the feedback from the focus groups' perspectives in the findings, and rank and recommend the competencies that require higher education support in the future.

3 RESULTS

3.1 Supply

In total, 160 respondents were contacted, of which 51% completed the survey, 5% partially completed the survey, 4% were discarded and 40% did not respond to the questionnaire. As a result, 84 valid answers were obtained from various higher education institutions in Scandinavia, including those offering master studies (52%), bachelor studies (18%), professional bachelor studies (6%), professions (17%) and others (7%). For the completed and partially completed responses, the country and gender distribution was as follows: Danish (63%) and Swedish (37%); female (22%) and male (78%) (Figure 1).

3.2 Demand

In total, 435 respondents were contacted, of which 18% completed the survey, 6% partially completed the survey, 3% were discarded and 72% did not respond to the questionnaire. As a result, 92 valid answers were obtained from industry, including architects (10%), building consultants (4%), consulting engineers (11%), daylight advisers (5%), from the energy sector (7%), lighting designers (21%), manufacturers (14%), municipalities (11%), sales (1%) and others (16%). For the completed and partially completed responses, the country and gender distribution was as follows: Danish (63%) and Swedish (37%); female (25%) and male (75%) (Figure 1).

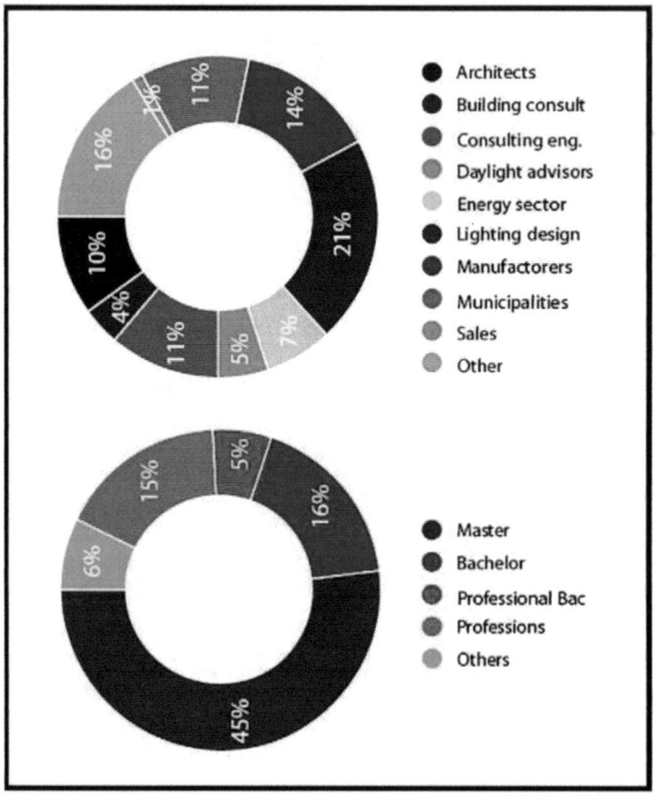

Figure 1: Survey responses based on educational level and sector

3.3 Crossing borders

To show the distribution of supply and demand, the survey participants were marked in red and blue, respectively, on the map of Denmark and Southern Sweden (Figure 2). Due to the size difference, five educational institutions in the northern part of Sweden, including two education institutions in Luleå, two in Umeå 2 and one in Sundsvall were not included in Figure 2. The graph shows that the concentration of lighting related competencies is currently highest in the larger cities, particularly in Greater Copenhagen.

https://doi.org/10.1051/shsconf/20184301004

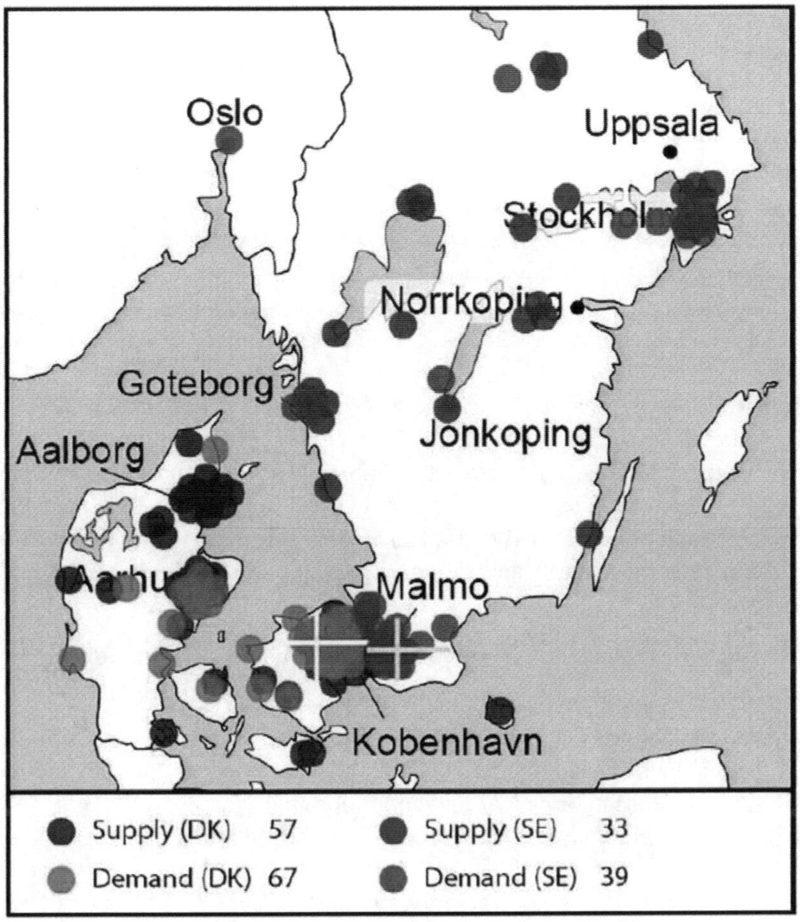

Figure 2: Geographic distribution of survey participants, divided into supply and demand. Red dots representing Danish answers and blue dots

3.4 Gaps – statistics

The results of the two online surveys are derived from the survey data and based on a Likert scale of 1-4, where 1 = not at all, 2 = to lesser degree, 3 = to some degree and 4 = to high degree. The additional option was provided to select "don't know" and add a qualitative comment. The "don't know" answers were discarded. All 111 categories included in the survey were investigated and the biggest gaps were identified and categorized by using descriptive analysis. To investigate these findings more thoroughly, we applied statistical analysis in the form of a Wilcoxon Signed-Rank test. Statistical significance supported the indication for the effect of the gaps, thereby, ensuring reliability of the obtained results and supporting the final categorization of the identified gaps between supply and demand.

3.5 Overview of competencies and categories

All results were compiled in a table (only partially reproduced in Figure 3) by combining all the information to provide an overview of all competencies and categories.

The first column of the table refers to the category of priority. Selected competencies were categorized with pink (high priority), orange (some priority), yellow (less priority) and white (no priority).

The second column indicates the characteristic of the gap: 'd' means the gap is large because the demand is very high (average >3), 's' is used when the supply is very low (average <2) and "d/s" is used when a competence has both a high demand and a low supply.

The third and fourth columns show a color code based on the average S (supply) and D (demand). Bright red (lowest <1.5) – yellow (average 2.25-2.5) – highest (dark blue >3.45) (Table 1, 2 of 2 for the entire scale).

The fifth column indicates how large the gap between the averages of supply and demand is. Green = good <0.75; white = okay 0.76-0.90; blue = not good; 0.91-1.24; pink = alarming > 1.25.

The next three columns show the findings of the statistical Wilcoxon ranked sum analysis. More red dots (1-3) equal bigger statistical evidence of the gap. (1) If Effect Size > 0.3 and either mean or mode have a measureable difference >2. (2) If the last test is true = if effect size >0.3 and supported by two measures = the difference in both mean and mode >2. (3) If the last test = true, supported by the two measures and effect size > 0.5.

The ninth and tenth columns refer to the name and number of the topics and competencies.

The columns eleven to thirteen rank the three educational levels with the highest supply in that category and the column fourteen the most frequent number in that topic.

The same applies to the columns seventeen to twenty, where the numbers refer to the sector with the highest demand. If the numbers are red, the supply/demand is very low all over. If the numbers are green, the demand is very high for all categories and maybe in more than three.

The last two columns, fifteen and sixteen, refer to the above-mentioned educational scores, but are related to the nationality, where red represents Denmark (DK) and blue represents Sweden (SE). A darker color shows that the supply/demand is convincingly higher in either DK or SE, while if the color is light, the supply/demand is higher, but not to the same degree.

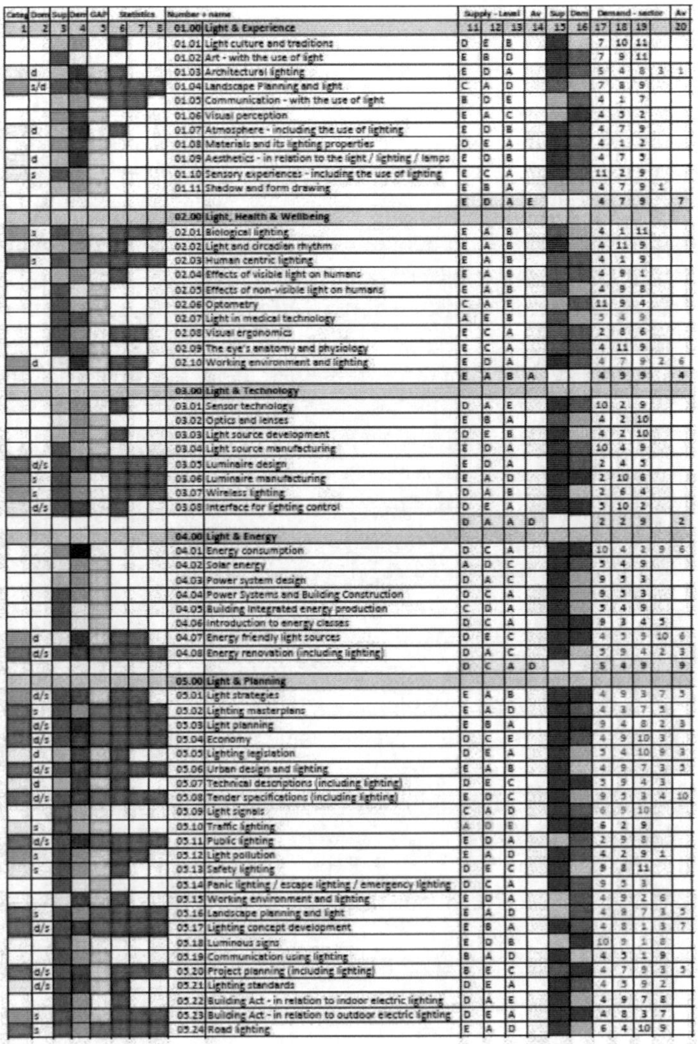

Categ	Dom	Sup	Dem	GAP	Statistics			Number + name		Supply - Level			Av	Sup	Dem	Demand - sector				Av
1	2	3	4	5	6	7	8	01.00	Light & Experience	11	12	13	14	15	16	17	18	19		20
								01.01	Light culture and traditions	D	E	B				7	10	11		
								01.02	Art - with the use of light	E	B	D				7	9	11		
	d							01.03	Architectural lighting	E	D	A				5	4	8	3	1
	s/d							01.04	Landscape Planning and light	C	A	D				7	8	9		
								01.05	Communication - with the use of light	B	D	E				4	1	7		
								01.06	Visual perception	E	A	C				4	5	2		
	d							01.07	Atmosphere - including the use of lighting	E	D	B				4	7	9		
								01.08	Materials and its lighting properties	D	E	A				4	1	2		
	d							01.09	Aesthetics - in relation to the light / lighting / lamps	E	D	B				4	7	5		
	s							01.10	Sensory experiences - including the use of lighting	E	C	A				11	2	9		
								01.11	Shadow and form drawing	E	B	A				4	7	9	1	
										E	D	A	E			4	7	9		7
								02.00	Light, Health & Wellbeing											
	s							02.01	Biological lighting	E	A	B				4	1	11		
								02.02	Light and circadian rhythm	E	A	B				4	11	9		
	s							02.03	Human centric lighting	E	A	B				4	1	9		
								02.04	Effects of visible light on humans	E	A	B				4	9	1		
								02.05	Effects of non-visible light on humans	E	A	B				4	9	8		
								02.06	Optometry	C	A	E				11	9	4		
								02.07	Light in medical technology	A	E	B				5	4	9		
								02.08	Visual ergonomics	E	C	A				2	8	6		
								02.09	The eye's anatomy and physiology	E	C	A				4	11	9		
	d							02.10	Working environment and lighting	E	D	A				4	7	9	2	6
										E	A	B	A			4	9	9		4
								03.00	Light & Technology											
								03.01	Sensor technology	D	A	E				10	2	9		
								03.02	Optics and lenses	E	B	A				4	2	10		
								03.03	Light source development	D	E	B				4	2	10		
								03.04	Light source manufacturing	E	D	A				10	4	9		
	d/s							03.05	Luminaire design	E	D	A				2	4	5		
	s							03.06	Luminaire manufacturing	E	A	D				2	10	6		
	s							03.07	Wireless lighting	D	A	B				2	6	4		
	d/s							03.08	Interface for lighting control	D	E	A				5	10	2		
										D	A	A	D			2	2	9		2
								04.00	Light & Energy											
								04.01	Energy consumption	D	C	A				10	4	2	9	6
								04.02	Solar energy	A	D	C				5	4	9		
								04.03	Power system design	D	A	C				9	5	3		
								04.04	Power Systems and Building Construction	D	C	A				9	5	3		
								04.05	Building integrated energy production	C	D	A				5	4	9		
								04.06	Introduction to energy classes	D	C	A				9	3	4	5	
	d							04.07	Energy friendly light sources	D	E	C				4	5	9	10	6
	d/s							04.08	Energy renovation (including lighting)	D	A	C				5	9	4	2	3
										D	C	A	D			5	4	9		9
								05.00	Light & Planning											
	d/s							05.01	Light strategies	E	A	B				4	9	3	7	5
	s							05.02	Lighting masterplans	E	A	D				4	3	7	5	
	d/s							05.03	Light planning	E	B	A				9	4	8	2	3
	d/s							05.04	Economy	D	C	E				4	9	10	3	
	d							05.05	Lighting legislation	D	E	A				5	4	10	9	3
	d/s							05.06	Urban design and lighting	E	A	B				4	9	7	3	5
	d							05.07	Technical descriptions (including lighting)	D	E	C				5	9	4	3	
	d/s							05.08	Tender specifications (including lighting)	E	D	C				9	5	3	4	10
								05.09	Light signals	C	A	D				6	9	10		
	s							05.10	Traffic lighting	A	D	E				6	2	9		
	d/s							05.11	Public lighting	E	D	A				2	9	8		
	s							05.12	Light pollution	E	A	D				4	2	9	1	
	s							05.13	Safety lighting	D	E	C				9	8	11		
								05.14	Panic lighting / escape lighting / emergency lighting	D	C	A				9	5	3		
								05.15	Working environment and lighting	E	D	A				4	9	2	6	
	s							05.16	Landscape planning and light	E	A	D				4	9	7	3	5
	d/s							05.17	Lighting concept development	E	B	A				4	8	1	3	7
								05.18	Luminous signs	E	D	B				10	9	1	8	
								05.19	Communication using lighting	B	A	D				4	5	1	9	
	d/s							05.20	Project planning (including lighting)	B	E	C				4	7	9	3	5
	d/s							05.21	Lighting standards	D	E	A				4	5	9	2	
								05.22	Building Act - in relation to indoor electric lighting	D	A	E				4	9	7	8	
	s							05.23	Building Act - in relation to outdoor electric lighting	D	E	A				4	8	3	7	
	s							05.24	Road lighting	E	A	D				6	4	10	9	

Figure 3: Comprehensive overview of analysis results (only partially reproduced here)

4 DISCUSSION

4.1 Pros and cons

Mapping the gaps between the educational supply on the one hand, and the demand from the interdisciplinary lighting industry, on the other, in both Denmark and Sweden proved to be very complex. Therefore, several decisions were made to both define and limit the study. These include a more precise definition of the employers (municipalities and industries) located in the Greater Copenhagen Region, while educational programs covered the entire area of Denmark and Sweden. This decision was made early in the study, considering the fact that employers do not necessarily rely on local education providers to obtain the knowledge they require. However, it may be argued that the education programs referred to in the study might be developed in the region with advantages to both education and employers. This discussion however goes beyond the scope of this study and remains within the remit of the overall Lighting Metropolis strategy.

Furthermore, the selection of the Likert Scale for collecting quantitative data proved to have both benefits and disadvantages. One of the benefits was the possibility to combine all 111 competencies into one questionnaire suitable for various types of respondents. This open approach allowed us to combine, within an almost identical questionnaire, various educational levels, institutions, courses, and systems into one group of respondents. It has also enabled us to combine a wide variety and size of "demanders" in the private and public sector, including municipalities, artists, international engineering companies, architect firms, salesmen and lighting designers, into the second group of respondents. In this way, the survey could embrace different types of respondents and accommodate the variety to be found in the context of the study.

Reaching a minimum of 80 participants from both groups was set as the target. While this target was in fact achieved, the supply-survey response rate was 51%, which despite personal phone calls and email correspondence was lower than the goal of 70% of the invited participants. This result may have been influenced by the inclusion of a long introduction text and 111 questions, some of which had little or no relevance for some respondents. Additional bias may have occurred because some relevant educational institutions did not participate in the study.

The Likert scale applied for the survey questions included the following measures , namely "high degree", "some degree", "lesser degree" and "not at all". To some degree, the respondents answered based on their subjective understanding of these levels, leading to the possibility of bias in the results. For example, one educator may have assigned the answer of "4 - supply to a high degree" to the inclusion of a 15 ECTS course in their curriculum, while another may have signed a similar value to a 5 ECTS course. The survey however intentionally ignored the measure of ECTS credits as the indicative of the supply, as the Danish Centre for Light previously attempted (Dansk Center for Lys & Innovationsnetværket Dansk Lys, 2012). This is primarily due to the fact that the questions and answers based on ECTS may be similarly misleading, as many aspects of lighting education can be found in the courses dealing with other subjects. One example is the area of light and energy, which can fall within broader approaches and coursework on sustainability. This may have forced the respondents to make subjective estimates of the share that lighting has in the total course.

4.2 Randomization

To keep the order of the themes and sub-points, all the participants answered the questions in the same order. In a longer survey such as this one, where we attempted to ensure the average answer time of eight minutes, participants may become impatient, annoyed or merely bored toward the end of the survey. If so, this can cause bias in the answers to the last themes compared to the first themes. In the partially completed answers, we see that especially the 'demand' participants tended to quit the survey in the middle of theme 5 "Light and planning". This can also indicate that the participants in online surveys lose concentration after approximately 50 questions.

4.3 Tendencies

When comparing the results and analysis from both surveys, the demand was higher than the supply for all 111 questions. This finding might suggest a tendency that the educational suppliers were more careful in their statement of what degree they educate in the different fields, and that people on the demand side exaggerate what they need and want from the people they employ. It may however also be interpreted that there is simply a higher demand than supply in all 111 categories. However, to accommodate this apparent imbalance, the gap between the supply and the demand is only considered significant when the difference between the average values is above 1.25 on the scale from 1-4 (Figure 3, row 5).

Another tendency suggests that the biggest suppliers of lighting-related education are among university colleges ("professions højskoler"), although an exception to this is the theme 4 "Light & Energy", where engineering programs supply is at a high level.

The highest demand varies over the eight themes (Figure 3, rows 11-13).

Looking at the geographical distribution of the supply based on the themes, there is a tendency towards a higher Danish supply across all themes with the exception of theme 2 "Health & Wellbeing", where the Swedish supply is higher and theme 8 "Characteristics and Measurements", where the distribution is more even.

The country-based demand is much more inconsistent, showing a strong tendency towards a higher Swedish demand in theme 1 "Experience", theme 2 "Health & Wellbeing" and theme 8 "Characteristics and Measurements" and a higher Danish demand in theme 4 "Light and Energy" and theme 6 "Daylight", as well as a small tendency in theme 7 "Digitalized light" (Figure 3, rows 15-16).

4.4 Implications

The gaps were divided into three categories based on the dominant factor responsible for the gap, i.e.: significantly low supply, higher than average demand or a combination of high demand and low supply (Figure 3, row 2). Additionally, all 111 categories were evaluated based on the gap size, statistical significance of gap and popularity. The most significant gaps were divided into three final categories that determine their priority (Figure 3, rows 3-8).

5 CONCLUSIONS

This study supports the findings of the previous studies, in particular the DCL-report published in 2012 (Dansk Center for Lys & Innovationsnetværket Dansk Lys, 2012), which indicated a high demand for interdisciplinary qualifications in Denmark and pointed out that the lighting industry was lacking specialized skills related to lighting design and that many companies were willing to offer internships and collaborative projects. The research on competencies, job functions and demand in the engineering field, performed by The Danish Technological Institute, suggested that in 2020 engineers that are able to work in a cross-disciplinary field will be in high demand (Teknologisk Institut, 2013). The present study qualifies and expands this previous research, providing a more in-depth analysis of the needs for future educational programs.

The statistical analysis of the surveys highlights the significant gaps between the supply and the demand. These areas and competencies were identified and categorized. The biggest gaps were located and systemized into three categories ('high', 'some', and 'less' priority) to provide a guidance for future action.

5.1 Primary priority

The areas with the largest gaps between the supply of education and the employment demand, categorized as the highest priority, are as follows. In the pink category, marked as high priority, we find 18 competencies from six different topics. Of these 18, eleven topics have a large gap based on the combination of low supply (average< 2) and high demand (average>3), whereas seven topics don't have a significantly high demand, but a very low level of supply (average<2).

1.04 Landscape Planning and Light: the supply is low, with the average of 1.7 and 57% answered "not at all" and the demand is high, with 94% of the answers stating the related demand and the average of 3.1.

2.03 Human Centric Lighting: There is an interest from the lighting industry, but the supply is very low. In total, 69% of the participants answered "not at all", while 85% require knowledge in this area, and the average is 2.9.

3.05 Luminaire Design: a skill that can be found in design and architecture. The supply is low, as 50% of the respondents answered "not at all", while the demand is high, with 89% of the answers stating the related demand and the average of 3.1.

4.08 Energy Renovation: for private and public buildings and for cities. The supply is low, as 52% of the respondents answered "not at all", while the demand is high, with 93% of the answers stating the related demand and the average of 3.2.

5.02 Lighting Master Plans: zooming out and taking a view from above. The supply is low, as 74% of the respondents answered "not at all", while the demand is average, with 87% of the answers stating the related demand and the average of 2.8.

5.03 Light Planning: in every project involving lighting design, lighting has to be planned in collaboration with architects, landscape, engineers etc. The supply is low, as 46% answered "not at all" while the demand is very high, with 97% of the answers stating the related demand and the average of 3.4.

5.04 Economy: very important in every business, but not as interesting from the research point of view. The supply is low, as 54% answered "not at all", while the demand is high, with 95% of the answers stating the related demand and the average of 3.2.

5.06 Urban Design and Lighting: lighting and landscape can be important for the image and growth of an area and a good opportunity to collaborate. The supply is low, as 62% answered "not at all", while the demand is high, with 92% of the answers stating the related demand and the average of 3.1.

5.08 Tender Specifications – including lighting: being able to read and understand specifications and project requirements is not an important part of the educational curriculum at most schools. The supply is low, as 46% answered "not at all", while the related demand is very high, with 95% of the answers stating the demand and the average of 3.3.

5.11 Public Lighting: the supply is low, as 53% answered "not at all", while the demand is very high, with 92% of the answers stating the related demand and the average of 3.3.

5.17 Lighting Concept Development: creativity and mastering new concepts. The supply is low, as 64% answered "not at all", while the demand is very high, with 97% of the answers stating the related demand and the average of 3.2.

5.20 Project Planning and Light: project management and planning is a skill that many employees need to have after they graduate. The supply is low, as 52% answered "not at all", while the demand is very high, with 93% of the answers stating the related demand and the average of 3.0.

5.24 Road Lighting: Keeping up with national standards for safety and illuminance, glare etc. The supply is very low, with the average of 1.4; 76% answered "not at all", and the demand is average with 80% of the answers stating the related demand and the average of 2.8.

5.25 Commissioning and Maintenance of Lighting: working in engineering companies and municipalities. The supply is very low, with the average of 1.7 and 72% answered "not at all" and the demand is average, with 86% of the answers stating the related demand and the average of 2.9.

7.10 Smart City: understanding IoT and what the collected data can be used for is a newly required skill. The supply is very low, with the average of 1.4 and 68% answered "not at all" and the demand is average, with 79% of the answers stating the related demand and the average of 2.5.

8.11 Evaluation of Luminaires and Light Sources: quality and post evaluation is in demand. The supply is low, as 61% answered "not at all", while the demand is very high, with 87% of the answers stating the related demand and the average of 3.1.

8.20 Light Sources – Aging and Degradation: the supply is low and 60% answered "not at all" and the demand is average, with 89% of the answers stating the related demand and the average of 2.9.

8.21 Calculation Software: using a range of calculation programs to test lighting concepts and show proof of specifications in a project. The supply is low, as 66% answered “not at all” and the demand is very high, with 88% of the answers stating the related demand and the average of 3.2.

5.2 Further recommendations

The study has identified the areas that require attention in order to bridge the gaps in the future. The gaps between, on the one hand, the competencies required by the employers and, on the other, the competencies provided through educational programs should be addressed through improving and expanding curricula at all levels of the educational system.

Furthermore, based on the discussions and debates in the expert interviews and focus groups carried out under this study, we further recommend that future educational curricula also take the following needs points into consideration:

- More interdisciplinary projects;
- More projects with external partners;
- Collaborations with public projects and internships at municipalities;
- The lighting industry needs more knowledge of the competencies in demand, when hiring new employees;
- Students should be aware of their opportunities in the labor market;
- Short courses for employee brush-up;
- Student “master class” in reading and understanding the required skills: standards, planning, legislation and other skills that students don’t get familiar with at university;
- Economy is also an important parameter.

The above priorities are important for educational programs and institutions to note in order to move towards generating research, knowledge and graduates who can meet the rapidly changing demands within the lighting industry and related fields.

6 Acknowledgements

The authors wish to express their gratitude to the participants of the surveys, interviews and focus groups who took their time to engage in the study. The authors received invaluable assistance on the statistical and mathematical analyses from their Aalborg University colleagues, Associate Professor Hendrik Purwins and Research Assistant Andreas Wulff-Jensen. The study described in this paper is a part of the project ‘Lighting Metropolis’, financed by Interreg.

7 References

Dansk Center for Lys, & Innovationsnetværket Dansk Lys. (2012). *Behov for lysuddannelse i Danmark*. København.

Schlangen, L. J. M., Lang, D., Novotny, P., Plischke, H., Smolders, K. C. H. J., Beersma, D. G. M., … Halonen, L. (2014). Lighting for health and well-being in education, work places, nursing homes, domestic applications and smart cities. https://doi.org/fp7-ict-2013-11-619249 accelerate
Teknologisk Institut. (2013). Den Danske ingeniør 2020 – Jobfunktioner og Kompetencekrav. Retrieved from https://www.teknologisk.dk/kompetencekrav-til-ingenioeren-i-2020/34048

Environmental identity: "space" vs "place"

Elena Lekus*

ITMO University, The Higher School of Lighting Design 190000 Grivtsova, 14, Saint Petersburg, Russia

Abstract. The article considers the problem of environmental identity, which is one of the most important criteria for the quality of the city's light environment. It is argued that a city's sustainable development means creating conditions for the process of identifying its inhabitants, transforming the concept of the city as a "space" into the concept of the city as a "place". There are a number of important socio-cultural trends that form the lighting culture of the modern city.

1 Luminous image

Since 90 percent of general information is communicated through sight, most information about an environment that a person receives is through light. Correspondingly, the entire world of objects and its sign-shaped system are an inexhaustible, though not the only, source of the human perception of reality. Lighting design's main function then becomes the illumination of the environment, which is responsible for the way that people see the world, its shapes, signs, symbols and meaning, in contrast to darkness.

"In service to the customer, lighting creates physical images and generates interpretations of lighting solutions. Lighting provides a clear spatial and social city life at night, identifying urban objects, their values, layouts, features and functions. It defines movement, specific points, options of stops and motion, orientation, static observation or dynamic play with visual perception [...]" [1].

Created by a specialist, the luminous image of this world may be similar to that which would be seen in natural daylight or have seemingly endless differences. In all cases, everything a person sees in an artificially lit space is the result of forming and producing light.

As Lynch noted, "the setting offers separation and dependency. As an observer, possessing a high degree of adaptability and on the basis of one's own needs, selects, organizes and gives value to what he sees" [2]. In this case, the perception of the urban environment in natural daylight is the topic of discussion. What changes to people's perceptions are caused by artificial light?

The luminous image is a "set of elements" of an original "day" object image or its constructing. In other words, the work to create a night-time image implies a selection or

* lekus_elena@mail.ru

analysis of a number of items visible in natural daylight, and their subsequent constructing or synthesis, using artificial light.

As a result, the "new", i.e. lighted object acquires a certain meaning and becomes a sign in accordance with the tasks established by a designer.

A viewer sees only the result of this work, thereby receiving an objective reality "filtered" by means of lighting. This means that artificial lighting forms an environment different from the daily one created by the city's sign-imaging system, as well as a different ontology and different identity. In fact, the lighting environment itself already exists as a new sign-imaging system, another objective reality, which, willingly or not, every citizen experiences after twilight.

How can one turn this environment into a harmonious "model" that has an identity with a close relationship to the modern person?

It seems that the answer to this question lies in the very nature of light and its ability to identify, illuminate and recognize specific forms of the surrounding reality, and create its new forms, images and meanings, as “light to a greater extent expresses ethical order [more] than words” [3].

2 Place Identity and Lighting Design

In the process of the multiculturalization of modern society, great importance is placed on preservation of national identity, as well as personal and collective identity. Light, which is responsible for the morphology of the city at night, allows one to select a dominant culture, to create direct links and put a symbolic emphasis on universal values. This feature is directly related to the creation of conditions for the formation of identity at different levels, such as national cultural identity, community identity, subcultural identity, and self-identity.

The modern world is experiencing many complex processes and issues: information overload, globalization and multiculturalism, clashes of ethnic and religious nature, social disintegration, the disintegration of former ideologies and worldviews, and the replacement of social roles. In such conditions, identification with anything becomes unstable or extremely short-lived.

“Environmental Identity” is one of the defining criteria when considering the quality of urban environmental design projects. This includes the city’s lighting environment.

What is “environmental identity”, which is sometimes called “place identity “and “place attachment”? What are the conditions, principles, and ways of transforming a “space” into a “place”? And what is the nature of the relationship between a person and an environment in this identification process? In the case of “environmental identity”, we are dealing immediately with two aspects of identification: the identity of a person and the identity of the place.

The concept “identity” and “identification” was borrowed by psychology project practitioners. In particular, E. Erikson considered identity in the context of psychosocial development and its different stages. Erickson defines ego-identity and group identity. Ego-identity is the deep internal structure of a person, which is responsible for the formation of a person’s integrity and continuity in their personality throughout their life. This category remains a constant, as it does not depend on the changes that occur within the person. Group identity is a feeling of inner unity with a social group, its ideals, values and ethical norms [4].

With the passage of time, there has been a significant transformation in the ideas surrounding a person’s underlying identity. If previously it had been viewed from the standpoint of different types of social identity (gender, age, nationality), today it acquires spatial and temporal characteristics. In other words, categories such as “atmosphere”, “situation”, “place spirit”, and “temporality” begin to play an increasingly important role in the formation of the urban environment. It is a kind of new turn in the development of the phenomenological approach to creating a space for human life.

Thus, the lighting design solves not only the traditional tasks (e.g. a sense of security and comfort, or energy saving), but also solves the problem of forming a place's identity. This means that the light environment creates such external conditions that allow a person to feel themselves a full "participant" of a particular environmental situation.

People need to be aware of themselves not only as a physical unit of a particular space, but also to feel mental, psychological and sensual-emotional involvement in a specific place, so that they consider themselves a "participant". This involvement is the result of the formation of a surrounding reality's holistic image.

In order to become such a "participant", a person needs to be aware of themselves not only as a physical unit of a particular space, but also to feel mental, psychological and sensual-emotional ownership of a specific place, which is created by forming an integral picture of the person's surrounding reality.

The formation of such a holistic image includes:

- Visual images that a person sees before themselves (the morphology of the city during day and night);
- Cultural symbols to which a person relates; and
- the psycho-emotional state of a person, which is born during the stay in the environment, i.e. the feeling of "involvement" in the environment and the processes occurring in it (interaction with the city and other people, self-determination, goal-setting, assimilation of ethical norms, traditions, way of life, etc).

Light cultures plays an important role in the formation of urban identity and the identity of the place, since light is an effective and "fast" tool for transforming and adapting the urban environment to the needs of the population, including the need for identification.

Light designers use different techniques to form an identity of the place. These include:

- Changing the spatial and temporal organization through lighting;
- The features of natural and climatic conditions, reflected in the design decision;
- The method of retrospection, and "awakening" the history of the place;
- The appeal to cultural traditions, customs, and social rituals;
- Analysis of social behaviours, the lifestyles, and social processes associated with the city or its fragment; and
- The involvement of the local population in the process of identifying the originality of the projected environment.

The range of lighting solutions to create the identity of a place is very large. These projects are both temporary and long-term. A good example is the project and reconstruction of the medieval harbor in Gent, Belgium. Thanks to the lighting design, the harbour has found a poetic and picturesque atmosphere, which is associated with the paintings of 19th century Dutch artists. The manifestation of the historical spirit (Latin, *genius loci*) transformed the deserted harbour into a vibrant cultural space, for people of all generations.

Another example is a specific illumination of the Old Town in Toronto, Canada. In accordance with the master development plan for the preservation and development of the city's historical heritage, the lighting project (2013) emphasizes the historical and cultural layers of space. The rest of the environment is a less illuminated background. As in the previous example, the emphasis in the coverage of the Old Town is on identifying the historical context as the basis for forming this place's identity [5].

A fundamentally different solution can be seen in the lighting of the Jacques Cartier Bridge in Montreal. This massive bridge with a simultaneously slender monumental structure starts to live a special life at night. Thanks to an innovative intelligent technological program, the light scenario of this bridge is associated with a large system of data (weather, traffic, social networks) and responds to changes in the data. Thus, the conceptual lighting project unites the bridge, the city and the townspeople and is an interactive identifier of city life.

São Paulo's lighting project, (2011-2012) conducted by Roger Narboni and Plinio Godoy, is an excellent example of the formation of place identity. The main goal of this project was the creation of a night landscape that expressed the historical and cultural identity of the Brazilian metropolis.

This industrial giant was the result of an amazing combination of architectural epochs, styles, and international cultural characteristics. It has numerous viaducts, tunnels and transitions that cannot cope with traffic congestion and which give a complex visual structure to the historical centre. At the same time the city's social life is most active at night.

The analysis of the urban situation showed that the existing coverage cannot meet the numerous needs of the city and its inhabitants [6]. The project was to unite all the historical and cultural diversity of the city and simultaneously show the monumentality of the night scenery.

The concept of a lighting masterplan was born from the history of the city. Previously, the historic centre of São Paulo crossed the river. This historical fact became the starting point for the creative intent of designers. "Invisible" rivers became the basis of the city's night image, which recreated the majestic natural landscape (Fig. 1,2).

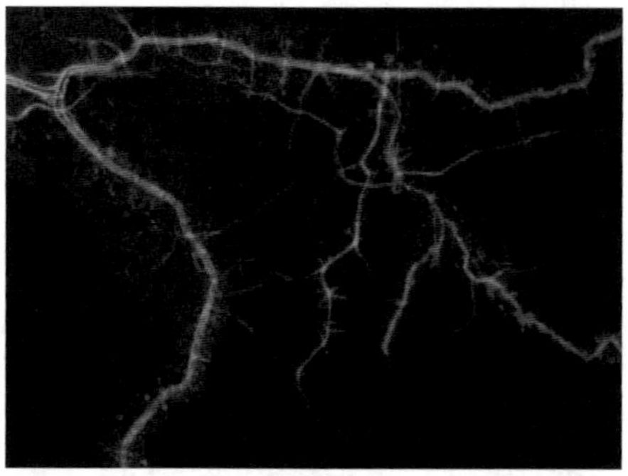

Fig.1. Narboni Roger & Plinio Godoy. São Paulo LMP. River nightscape map.

Fig. 2. Narboni Roger & Plinio Godoy. São Paulo. Praza da Se computer rendering.

Another project that which is a good example of the creation of place identity is the upgrade of the Novosmolenskaya embankment in Saint-Petersburg, Russia. The project "Development of a model of the lighting environment for St. Petersburg" was implemented by St. Petersburg State Unitary Enterprise "Lensvet" and The Higher School of Lighting Design ITMO University within the framework of the "integrated programme for the development of St. Petersburg as a centre of light culture for the period 2018-2030 and up to 2050".

The architectural ensemble of the Novmoslenskaya embankment was created relatively recently in 1970-1980. In the original project, the embankment was projected from the shore of the Gulf of Finland. The grandiose ensemble was conceived as a glorification of the idea of the Great October Revolution. In 1976, the city government planned the erection of a majestic monument dedicated to this significant event of Soviet history. The monument was to be located on a specially created island at the mouth of the Smolenka River, which subsequently gave the name of the embankment. However, this plan was not implemented. The turn of history was accomplished, the grandiose plan remained in the past and the ensemble has not been completed.

St. Petersburg is one of the few cities in the world that was created not spontaneously, but was instead consciously planned. The principle of the ensemble was originally the essence and the basis of this city.

In the case of the Novosmolenskaya embankment, the ensemble had to play an aesthetic role and an ideological role. However, the architectural environment of the Novosmolenskaya embankment had already been created, and the ideology has changed. For almost forty years this part of the city remained stagnant, giving birth to a feeling of incompleteness and unrealized potential of the place. Therefore, light designers face a complex task. The light solution should substantially change the morphology of the embankment at night and create its holistic individual image.

Within six months, the team of the lighting designers analysed the behavioural scenario, the nature of the interaction of residents with the space, and their relationship to the environment (Fig. 3).

Fig. 3. The Higher School of Lighting Design ITMO University & St. Petersburg State Unitary Enterprise "Lensvet". Lighting support the Novosmolenskaya embankment.

An integrated approach was used in the project of embankment lighting: it combined the aesthetic and functional aspects. The lighting solution emphasized the architectural ensemble of the Novosmolenskaya embankment. It was created as a line that connects the city with the water space of the Gulf of Finland. Lighting designers focused on a unique architectural environment of the Novosmolenskaya embankment and needs of citizens at night time. Experts proposed several solutions, and the people and the city administration chose the best of them. The result of this multi-faceted project included the interests of the city as a cultural and historic centre, oriented towards the future and needs of the residents.

Lighting emphasizes different levels of territory and creates the effect of a "deep" and multifunctional space. Less intense light is designed for the lower (promenade) zone for a comfortable rest on the river bank. The upper zone gets more intensive light, because the greatest activity of the inhabitants is in this part of the embankment.

The light plan includes two modes of everyday and festive lighting. Everyday lighting creates a characteristic atmosphere for St. Petersburg, which aids walks, socializing, and rest. O significant dates, light acquires a thematic character and enhances the festive event's spirit (Fig. 4, 5).

Fig. 4. The Higher School of Lighting Design ITMO University & St. Petersburg State Unitary Enterprise "Lensvet". Bridge Shipbuilders on the Novosmolenskaya embankment.

Fig. 5. The Higher School of Lighting Design ITMO University & St. Petersburg State Unitary Enterprise "Lensvet". Making the Novosmolenskaya embankment in the New Year.

This lighting project solves the complex problem of integrating the space of the Novosmolenskaya embankment into the historically developed space of the city. At the same time, lighting creates a "spirit of a place" and fills this space with the vital energy of people at night time.

In conclusion, we can say that identity in a changing world is one of the most important problems of modern society. Place identity and the identification of a person within a place are some of the most serious and important tasks to consider in light design. The criterion of identity is an indicator of a modern city's high level of light culture and is simultaneously an integral part to a sustainable city.

References

J.M. Deleuil, J.Y. Toussaint. Les annals de la recherché urbaine **87**, 56 (2000)
K. Linch. City image. 19 (1982)
J.M. Deleuil, J.Y. Toussaint. *Les annals de la recherché urbaine* **87** (2000)
E. H. Erikson. Childhood and Society (1963)
Heritage Lighting Master Plan For Old Town Toronto, by Toronto Heritage Preservation Services. 2011. Available at: www1.toronto.ca/city_of_toronto/city_planning/urban_design/files/pdf/hert_final_report.pdf (accessed 4 June 2017).
R. Narboni. Les éclairages des villes (2012)

Creating identity with nature inspired lighting design – The Sensitive Organism

Anna-Rosa Hiort-Lorenzen[1], *Beáta E.* Kublik[2], *Gordon* Jäntsch[3], *Paulina M.* Dudkiewicz[4] and *Georgios* Triantafyllidis (Supervisor)[5]

Master of Lighting Design, Department of Architecture, Design, and Media Technology, Faculty of Engineering and Science, Aalborg University Copenhagen, Denmark, 2017

Abstract. People, as living organisms, exist in symbiosis with nature; therefore, contact with nature is a basic human need. City nature is an important aspect of the urban living environment because people need an escapist experience from the everyday city life that they should find within their close environment. The outdoor lighting of urban nightscapes has a major influence on people's perception of space. Cities with an increasing number of inhabitants and late-night economic activity transform into 24-hour operating cities. This means that more attention should be given to investigating the social needs of public spaces in terms of night-time urban lighting, creating experiences and identities with nature. This paper aims to emphasize the potential hidden in nature-inspired lighting as a topic for further development in the field of lighting design. Nature inspired lighting is based on a transdisciplinary approach, where terms like biomimicry, biophilia, and urban green space adopted from other subject fields than lighting influence the lighting design process in order to create a product addressing human inner connectedness to nature. The example used in this paper presents the concept of a lighting master plan called "The Sensitive Organism".

1 Anna-Rosa Hiort-Lorenzen: ahiort16@student.aau.dk

2 Beáta E. Kublik: bkubli16@student.aau.dk

3 Gordon Jäntsch: gjaent16@student.aau.dk

4 Paulina M. Dudkiewicz: pdudki16@student.aau.dk

5 Georgios Triantafyllidis: gt@create.aau.dk

1 Introduction

Various studies have been carried out to examine the relationship between nature and lighting. The authors of this paper formulated conclusions based on two specific research activities, which are important for nature-inspired lighting design. The overall findings, used in the exemplary project – The Sensitive Organism, are briefly presented in this paper.

Natural scenes at exterior public spaces are perceived as having higher restorative quality. When natural objects are emphasized by light at night-time instead of man-made objects, these spaces are perceived to have more restorative quality [1], and changing the focus of the light in nightscapes can have similar effects on perceived restorativeness, fear and preference as changing the actual content of the scene. Illuminating artificial surfaces (e.g. asphalt pathways) with natural light patterns can enhance the presence of nature and, thus, increase the feeling of well-being.

Another research [2] investigated whether there is a more positive evaluation for the irregularity of a façade and daylight pattern in a social, rather than a working context. Three rendering scenes with different façade patterns were used by stereoscopic scene for virtual reality glasses in the experiment. Subjective evaluations of virtual space were recorded across six variations of façade pattern and sky types. The obtained evidence shows that pattern characteristics have an impact on the perceived spatial ambience with a preference for irregularity.

2 State of the Art

For nature inspired lighting, nature and its characteristics provide the main source of inspiration for the design. The aim goes beyond highlighting the existing nature in a favourable way. Such design should support the relationship between humans and nature, thus a preliminary study of basic terms describing this particular relationship is required. Three main terms, considered by the authors fundamental and relevant for the understanding of the context as well as the requirements and challenges of nature-inspired lighting, are analysed below.

a) The term Biophilia, introduced in 1973 by Erich Fromm, claims that humans possess an innate tendency to connect with nature and other forms of life [3]. Originally, Fromm described it as "the passionate love of life and of all that is alive". In 1984, Edward O. Wilson developed and popularised the idea through his work "Biophilia" and concluded that this affiliation might partly have a genetic basis [4]. Nowadays, people spend more and more time indoors, including buildings, cars and man-made parts of the environment. The lack of biophilic activities and the time spent in the nature can strengthen the disconnectedness of humans from nature. Therefore, effort must be put into the reestablishment of the relationship between humans and nature on a day-to-day basis. Previous research has proved that biophilia has a positive impact on productivity, lowering the level of stress, enhancing learning comprehension and creativity, and accelerating recovery from illness [5].

b) Biomimicry, also called biomimetics, is an approach that defines innovation as a search for sustainable solutions to human challenges in emulating nature time-tested patterns and strategies [6]. This approach assumes that nature can provide working solutions to the sustainability problems humans caused and are now struggling with. Years of evolution and adaptation to change proved nature's strong ability to survive despite the challenges. The term "biomimicry" was coined in 1982, but was popularized by scientist and author Janine Benyus in the late 20th century [7], who suggested looking at nature as a "Model, Measure and Mentor", that is, the largest laboratory that has ever existed and ever will. The article titled "Biomimetics: Design by Nature" published in *National Geographic* referred to biomimicry as the future of engineering [8].

c) Urban Green Space is a sub-part of urban open space, which contains all spaces accessible to the public within a city. A definition by Marilyn Myers from 1975 holds that as the counterpart of development, urban open space is a natural and cultural resource, synonymous with neither "unused land" nor "park and recreation areas" [9]. Urban green spaces represent a fundamental component of any urban ecosystem and include places, such as parks, woods, squares, gardens, and natural meadows as well as water elements ranging from ponds to coastal zones. Contrary to undisturbed natural areas outside the city, one of the urban nature's prominent features is its typical fragmentation into multiple small zones. Urban green areas play various roles in the urban environment. In particular, they increase the aesthetics of the city, provide space for recreation and preserve urban biodiversity. Contact with nature has a direct impact on physical, psychological, and social well-being [10] and such beneficial exposure can be provided to city inhabitants through urban green spaces.

The next step is to translate those definitions into the overall guidelines for lighting design. Biophilia tells us that people are attracted to nature. A more in-depth study of the variety of colours, shapes, materials, and movements in nature can be a source of inspiration for light projects in terms of both quality of light provided and the design of the luminaire. Innate human connection to nature places value upon nature and this can potentially add value to a design which mimics nature. Mimicking the nature with light can be an effective solution for urban areas with limited access to nature, and an interim way to offer experience and comfort to people whose biophilic needs are not fulfilled within their neighbourhood.

Biomimicry encourages the use of solutions that already exist in nature with the aim to create sustainable designs. Sustainability is a rising concern over the last decades and lighting design should address this issue, not only by achieving a watt-per-square-metre target. The LED revolution in the last decades contributes to significant energy savings, but sustainability should be considered in the entire lighting system, not only in the choice of the light source. Inspiration from biological solutions, from nano to macro scale, can possibly enhance lighting design in terms of its lifespan, maintenance, quality, aesthetics, energy consumption, and manufacturing costs.

Urban green spaces can be a canvas for lighting designers to contribute to the challenge of reconnecting people living in cities to nature. Proper lighting design should encourage people to use public green spaces, ensure the appropriate level of safety after the sunset and create a recreational atmosphere. While thinking of green areas, people tend to associate them with flora; however, it is important to consider an equally crucial part of nature, that is, fauna. Lighting design should support urban biodiversity, respecting flora and fauna as two coexisting elements of the urban ecosystem.

https://doi.org/10.1051/shsconf/20184301006

3 Project description

3.1 Context

This case study is part of a master plan developed for a public housing area in Copenhagen, Denmark, called "Urbanplanen Syd". As Nordic countries are exposed to long, dark winter days, it is essential to put emphasis on the night-time lighting. The task was to create a lighting design solution that meets specific social requirements of the local community.

Urbanplanen Syd was built in the 1960s for families from a densely populated area of Copenhagen to offer more space and nature in a healthier surrounding. Apart from residential buildings, the area has a church, school, library and a park. In the past years, the initial vision of the area frayed, as it got a bad reputation in media; therefore, the Municipality of Copenhagen announced a competition to solve the problem by reshaping the area (Fig. 1).

3.2 New Architectural Concept

The refurbishment plan aims for a new, sustainable neighbourhood based on three core values. The first element is the Games and learning platform offering children and adolescents room for both fun and games, while also creating prerequisites for acquiring and gaining new knowledge as part of so-called "learning landscapes". The second element is the Community, a district of relations, involving both the large and close community. In the close community, the most important resource is the neighbour and there is always a possibility for people of different age, gender and ethnicity to meet on equal terms. And the third element is City nature, a green context, that is never too far to get an experience of green surroundings. Nature, in this proposal, sets the scene for the everyday life in Urbanplanen Syd.

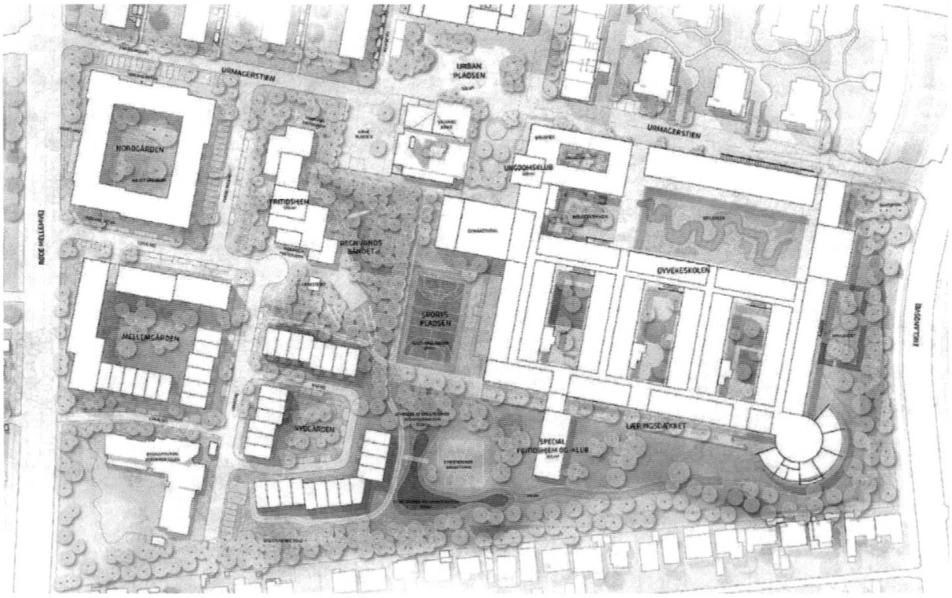

Fig 1. A new concept map introduced by the responsible architect "Tredje Natur" [11]

The task was to respond to the context and present a new architectural concept with a new, meaningful lighting design solution.

3.3 Problem of the Space

The solution to the existing problem requires an in-depth investigation of the issue. The design process, in this case, involves a multi-disciplinary study of the space, its inhabitants and the architecture in the current situation, as the new plans are not applied yet.

Looking at the problems that face the space at the moment in combination with the related solutions proposed by the architects, three main issues stand out: the unused potential of nature, the deteriorating reputation and the lack of integration between different nationalities living in the area. These problems are solved with the creation of a new common identity in architecture. This perception has to be maintained in the dark hours. Lighting that brings people closer to nature can establish a recreative, escapist experience during the night for metropolitans in big cities. As this lighting project is primarily focusing on creating a meaningful lighting experience, attention should be paid to involving people in a qualitative research based on what they consider pleasant, nature-driven stimuli in a public space.

4 Design Research

The concept is built upon criteria that focus on the values of city nature through the creation of a nature-driven light experience by researching the appropriate qualities of nature that can be transformed into light qualities. Based on the criteria, the design research focuses on the analysis of nature-inspired lighting solutions and natural phenomena in order to get a better understanding of the following design parameters:

- Natural textures
- Organic patterns
- Natural light sources
- Natural movements
- Interaction with people
- Environmental interactions

The project refers to theories formulated by William Lam and William H. Whyte, using their guidelines in the design selection. Lam describes the functional and biological needs of people – orientation, discernibility and communication [12]. Whyte introduces the term of triangulation – a process by which some external stimulus provides a linkage between people and prompts strangers to talk to each other. This stimulus can be a physical object or sight (musician, performer, sculpture) [13].

Several urban lighting design projects aimed to improve the perception of public spaces. The Dutch lighting project called Broken Light helped change the reputation of a neighbourhood in Rotterdam by involving nature and dynamic light into the light experience [14]. By researching how light is perceived and experienced in public spaces beyond street lighting regulations, it showed that a lighting concept is not just a matter of perception, but also an enabler for the identity of a space.

The transformation was beyond aesthetic - illuminating horizontal and vertical surfaces, and creating a natural "underwater-like" moving pattern on the street, helped to tackle the issues of crime and prostitution that used to demote the neighbourhood through a strengthened sense of community.

5 Lighting Concept

Next, a short description of the specific master plan is provided to demonstrate how nature inspired lighting design might be applied to a specific area. Considering that The Sensitive Organism was only developed as a concept, all presented solutions are theoretical and have not yet been scientifically tested. In general, this master plan provides guidelines for a specific residential area in Copenhagen, but is also appropriate for other areas with similar conditions.

5.1 The Sensitive Organism

The concept arises from the organic shape of the area, envisioned as a structure which reacts to incentives, that is, a sensitive organism. It cares for people's needs, supports their activities and occasionally comes with surprises for the inhabitants. Even though it is an abstract structure, it has three beating hearts in the centre of the area, it has veins along the main flows of people and it has organs in every place people gather and locate their activities.

The Sensitive Organism, as a visionary guideline, helps define the key aspects of the master plan and ensures the conceptual consistency, which is important for building a strong identity through the light.

5.2 The Raindrop Pattern

Guided by this nature inspired vision, the main visual feature of the lighting design was adopted from the movement occurring when raindrops encounter a water surface (Fig 2). The emerging, randomly placed, shapes create a dynamic pattern of multiple concentric circles with its own peculiar rhythm.

Fig 2. Typical raindrop pattern on a water surface

Translating this pattern into a light language, the shape and rhythm define the spatial light distribution. Thereby, every concentric ripple caused by a drop is represented by a spotlight from a luminaire above. According to the ripple propagation, the spot radius and brightness follow the same rhythm of the fading concentric wave. That means a static mounted spotlight projects a spot on the ground. The initial diameter is small and gradually expands within a specific time frame. While the diameter is increasing, the brightness is decreasing until zero. Finally, the small initial diameter quickly fades in and the cycle starts again. Unlike the rain, where one falling drop creates a series of concentric circles of different diameters, visible at once, one luminaire can produce only one circle at the time. Unlike the real rain pattern, only a few spots increase their radius, while their brightness is fading out to avoid an inappropriate, exaggerated visual dynamic. Most of the spots are at rest. To ensure a proper balance and create a pleasant natural, yet dynamic pattern, the spots have different initial rest diameters (Fig. 3). There is only a determined amount of used diameters extracted from the Fibonacci series of numbers [15]. This specific range is often found in natural growth processes or proportions. The chosen diameters are 3, 5, 8 and 13 meters which are used for the patterns.

Fig 3. An example of the initial raindrop spot pattern

5.3 Differentiated Parts of the Area

The raindrop pattern is used for the whole area but in different variations depending on the sub-area. These sub-areas are defined by specific features corresponding to the needs of the city dwellers. These features or how they are structured and used by people create the unique atmosphere of the area. At night, the light can enhance these effects and, thus, underline its identity. In this example, there are five sub-areas, namely major and minor paths, as well as major and minor squares and parks.

The atmosphere of the paths areas is characterized by its liveliness, a high degree of communication and, therefore, exudes a higher brightness.

The squares combine a public and private atmosphere. In addition, the main squares also have attraction points, like a fountain or an art installation, to entice people. At the same time, these places have more private parts at the periphery, where people could observe each other or engage in a conversation. The minor areas for both paths and squares are always a bit more private than the major ones.

In turn, the parks are defined in this example as having the most private and relaxing atmosphere due to the fact that they have the biggest amount of natural elements.

5.4 Parameters of a Pattern

Each of the sub-areas is assigned an appropriate pattern in order to enhance their atmosphere. Thereby, the patterns are distinguished by the composition of the following features:

A: A range of initial spot diameters used in one pattern

B: Density of spots in the entire pattern

C: The initial brightness level of entire pattern

D: The luminous texture of the spot area in the entire pattern

Regarding A, three different ranges of diameters are used to create three kinds of patterns. The first pattern consists of all diameters (13, 8, 5, 3 meters), the second excludes the smallest diameter (13, 8, 5 meters) and the third exclude the biggest diameter (8, 5, 3 meters). In this way, it is possible to achieve different scales of patterns. The bigger scale is suitable for a more public atmosphere whereas a smaller one is better for a cosy atmosphere [16]. Furthermore, as mentioned above the spots in some areas are dynamic. However, the biggest diameter of each range always remains static in order to ensure a good spatial orientation.

Regarding B, the density of spots corresponds to the distance between the spots within the entire pattern. Two different levels of density are used: a high level, corresponding to the distance of five meters, and a low level of three meters. As a result, a high-density pattern has a higher uniformity of illumination than a lower-densed one. Higher uniformity is suitable for a more public atmosphere, whereas lower uniformity better suits a cosy atmosphere [16].

Regarding C, two levels of horizontal illuminance in the entire master plan are used for a pattern that separates predominantly public areas from primarily private areas. A high illuminance level is assigned to public spaces and a low level to private ones. The high level should not exceed 10 lux. The existing scientific research points to the fact that the feeling of security increases with an average increase in the lighting level up to ca. 30 lux and that a small increase in illuminance up to 10 lux results in a large increase in perceived security [17].

Regarding D, the luminous texture of a spot describes the distribution of lighter and darker parts within the spot surface. Three different spot surfaces are used: a plain one, which contains no texture; a rippled texture similar to the ripples of a raindrop wave; and an organic texture with a caustic appearance (Fig. 4). The plain and rippled textures are used for the whole pattern, whereby the latter one creates a cosier atmosphere. The organic texture is only used for a single spot to serve as an eye-catcher.

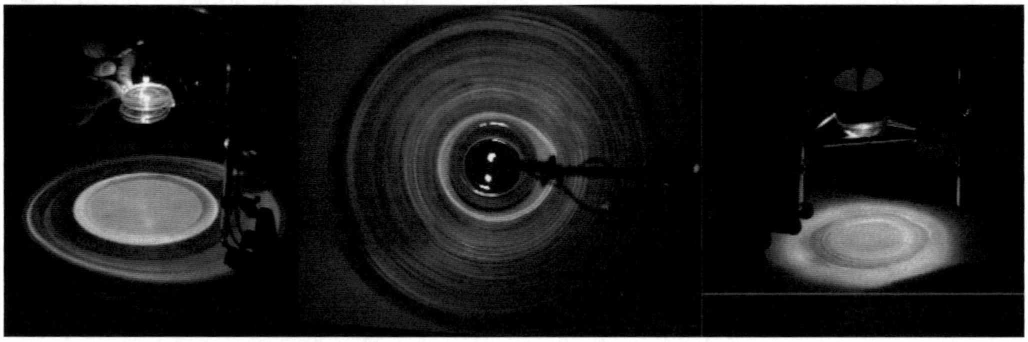

Fig 4. Three textures used: plain, ripple and organic

5.5 Further Variations of a Pattern

Other conceivable possibilities to adapt the pattern in order to enhance the appropriate atmosphere are the colour temperature and the height of the luminaire. A slow fade from a high to a low colour temperature may signalize the change from twilight until night and even at night, it can support a better temporal orientation.

The height of the luminaires can be adapted to the initial diameters of the spots. Whereby, the smaller the spot the lower the height is. The height of a light source towards the eye level influences the feeling of public sphere and privacy [18].

Furthermore, the speed of fading during one cycle of the raindrop rhythm can separate a quiet area from a lively one.

5.6 Application of the Patterns to the Areas

Major and minor paths are the veins of the Sensitive Organism. The big light spots of the pattern are situated in the middle of the street and the smaller ones in the periphery to illuminate elements like benches, bike parking, trees and facades. Trees and facades are illuminated to enhance the verticals.

Major and minor squares are the organs, whereby the attractions situated on the major squares are the hearts of the Sensitive Organism. Although the major squares have a very public atmosphere and, thus, require a high brightness, the chosen level of brightness is low in order to enhance the contrast with the bright attraction elements. These special elements are lit by one organic spot in order to provide a contrast with the texture.

The parks are intended to be the lungs of the Sensitive Organism. With a lower brightness of the pattern, lower density and the choice for smaller diameters and rippled texture, these areas are expected to have the greatest contrast with the previous ones. They create the most private and intimate place for people.

In Table 1, an overview of all pattern parameters is shown in order to illustrate the change from public to private atmosphere from left to right.

Table 1. Overview pattern parameters according to the areas

	Sub areas					
Feature	**Major paths**	**Minor paths**	**Major squares**	**Minor squares**	**Attractions on squares**	**Parks**
A: Range	13 - 8 - 5	13 - 8 - 5 - 3	13 - 8 - 5	13 - 8 - 5 - 3	13	8 - 5 - 3
B: Density	high	low	high	low	-	low
C: Brightness	high	low	low	low	high	low
D: Texture	plain	plain	plain	plain	organic	ripple

5.7 Horizontal and Vertical Illumination

Another recommendation of the master plan is the illumination of the whole field of view in order to enhance the readability of the space. This includes the illumination of horizontal as well as vertical surfaces of the environment.

The horizontal plane, involving the streets and pavements, is characterized by the raindrop pattern. It evenly covers the whole plane and is not coordinated with the geometry of the street grid. The aim is to create a natural organic view without emphasizing the straight built environment.

The vertical planes are formed by facades, trees and bushes. They are illuminated by grazing light. At the same time, natural elements are enhanced, which also increases the feeling of security [1].

5.8 Fixtures and Mounting

For this concept customized fixtures are necessary. Almost each fixture needs to be able to change its beam angle dynamically. This technology is already used in stage luminaries. Due to the relatively narrow beam angles, it might be possible to make the luminaires glare free. This technique is important to guide the view of the pedestrian on the floor rather than in the direction of the luminaire. This would be a vast change in the perception of public lighting, as nowadays street lighting is mostly not able to achieve this.

Furthermore, to generate different light textures, the fixtures should be equipped with specially treated lenses or gobos.

Due to multiple fixtures, an installation on tensed horizontal wires across the area reduces the number of polls. In addition, it provides a higher flexibility in the alignment of the fixtures in order to achieve the desired patterns.

In order to keep the maintenance of the luminaires low, it is recommended to use long-life LEDs and to avoid possible mechanical movement of lenses. Here further development steps are necessary.

5.9 Interaction Scheme

The Sensitive Organism was developed to create a natural identity at night in order to encourage passers-by to stay longer outside and enjoy contact with each other. People talking on the street may attract others to join the conversation. Supporting this behaviour also for people approaching from a bit more far away light is able to signalize speaking people to them. Using the dynamic light cycle of the raindrop idea in between a static light pattern may attract people because moving light always attracts attention.

By equipping the luminaire with a sound sensor, it will be possible to track talking people and trigger the dynamic drop cycle. After tracking, with the help of an interlinked controlling system, the adjacent spots start to run the cycle, too, in between a radius of about 20 meters. Once these talking people leave the place, the dynamic light fades away into the initial static pattern.

But the organism does not only react to people's behaviour but also to seasonal changes of the natural light in order to create a harmonic transition from day to night. The twilight duration can influence the fading time of the whole artificial light after sunset. Even the colours of the sunset can control the colours of the patterns during the night. To elaborate on this topic, further investigations are necessary and can be discussed in another paper.

5.10 Lighting Concept Summary

In conclusion, to illuminate a space in order to create natural identity the concept makes use of the idea of patterns, following the Fibonacci row, textures similar to ripples and organic caustics and natural rhythms, expressed by cycles of dynamic spot diameters and brightness.

To generate a real-time sensitivity to the organism concept, an interaction scheme can be implemented to influence the behaviour of the pedestrians.

6 Conclusion

The project "The Sensitive Organism" was an attempt to use light as a tool for enhancing the city nature and thus bringing inhabitants closer to each other by giving them space with a strong identity during night-time. This paper reflects substantial interest in the topic, where a case project was presented mainly to inspire the reader for its own further investigation, as the main focus should be placed on the overall potential of highlighting the nature in our design. Besides being aesthetic, nature-inspired lighting design can address human biophilic needs of having contact with nature on a daily basis. It can be done directly, by leading people with light into green spaces within the urban environment, or indirectly by mimicking nature with light, like 'The Sensitive Organism" project did with the rain ripples. Cities are getting bigger and nature is often polluted, so light is an "easy" way to create natural experience and change appearance without any significant intervention into architecture. Biomimicry goes even further by looking at nature as a source of solutions that are not only pleasant for people but are sustainable, of high quality and can last long, as nature proved to be able to survive all kind of changes including environmental challenges.

Benefits offered by nature are unlikely to be realized without a conscious decision of designers to enhance the presence of nature in cities and connect people to the surrounding nature.

7 Acknowledgement

The lighting design "The Sensitive Organism" was created as a group semester project in the framework of the lighting design master programme at Aalborg University Copenhagen in collaboration with the municipality of Copenhagen, tredje architecture and jaja architecture Copenhagen, who provided the authors with the material for the residential area of Urbanplanen Syd in Copenhagen.

8 References

[1] Heli Nikunen & Kalevi M. Korpela, The effects of scene contents and focus of light on perceived restorativeness, fear and preference in nightscapes, Journal of Environmental Planning and Management, Vol 55, No.4, 453-468, 2012

[2] Kynthia Chamilothori, Jan Wienold & Marilyn Andersen. Daylight patterns as a means to influence the spatial ambiance: a preliminary study, Interdisciplinary Laboratory of Performance-integrated Design (LIPID) Ecole polytechnique fédérale de Lausanne (EPFL), Switzerland, 2016

[3] biophilia, https://www.britannica.com/science/biophilia-hypothesis, downloaded December 2017

[4] E.O. Wilson, Biophilia, Harvard University Press, 1984

[5] Kellert, S. R., Heerwagen, J., & Mador, M. L. Biophilic Design: The Theory, Science, and Practice of Bringing Buildings to Life, published 2008

[6] Biomimicry, https://biomimicry.org/, downloaded December 2017

[7] What is Biomimicry, http://environment-ecology.com/biomimicry-bioneers/367-what-is-biomimicry.html, downloaded December 2017

[8] Biomimetics, http://ngm.nationalgeographic.com/2008/04/biomimetics/tom-mueller-text, downloaded December 2017

[9] Marilyn. "Decision Making in Allocating Metropolitan Open Space: State of the Art." Transactions of the Kansas Academy of Science 1975. pp 149–153.

[10] Keniger et al. 2013, Hough 2014

[11] Tredje Natur; https://www.urbanplanen.com/urbanplanen-syd?lightbox=dataItem-j03v25r6, downloaded December 2017

[12] Lam, William M., C., "Perception and Lighting as form-givers for Architecture",1977

[13] Whyte, William.H, "The Social Life of Small Urban Spaces" 1980

[14] "Broken Light", https://www.alanod.com/en/projects/broken-light/, downloaded 2017

[15] Fibonacci, http://www.maths.surrey.ac.uk/hosted-sites/R.Knott/Fibonacci/fibnat.html , downloaded 2017

[16] Lam, William M., C., "Perception and Lighting as form-givers for Architecture",1977

[17] Boyce PR, Eklund NH, Hamilton BJ, Bruno LD. Perceptions of safety at night in different lighting conditions. Lighting Research and Technology 2000; 32: 79–91.

[18] Descottes Hervé, "Architectural Lighting. Designing with Light and Space". Princeton Architectural Press, NY, 2011

The impact of restorative audio-visual environment learning on the stress

Nikolai Matveev [1], *Kirill* Shamritskiy[1]

[1]The St.-Petersburg ITMO UNIVERSITY

Abstract. The experiment, conducted in the laser theater Lux Aeterna on the basis of the ITMO University, was aimed at testing the hypothesis about the positive effect of dynamic audio-visual content on the psycho-emotional state of a person and her academic progress after a long period of exposure. Both groups underwent a lengthy Bourdon test and a Shcherbatyh test for the learning stress. Only the participants who passed the laser theater session improved their productivity in the performance of monotonous work in the further passage of the test and showed a significant decrease in the level of general learning stress at the end of the experiment. Correlations between the level of learning stress and academic progress were not found. The use of sessions of dynamic audio-visual content based on the laser theater Lux Aeterna can be considered as an alternative relaxation method that allows changing the level of learning stress in people, increasing productivity in the performance of monotonous work and improve general well-being.

1 Introduction

Over the last decade a significant number of studies were conducted in order to explore the influence of light on the human body [1, 2, 3]. Static artificial light can influence the psycho-emotional and psycho-physiological state of a person, both in a positive and negative way. [3].

In their everyday life people are exposed to dynamic lighting and changing visual content both in cities (e.g. advertising banners, a flickering lighting of shops and public buildings) and at home (e.g. screens of electronic devices). Daily exposure to such an environment can provoke of rapid fatigue, reduced efficiency, as well as stress and depression. And also it has a detrimental effect on the physiological health [1]. To reduce the negative impact of these factors, there are various techniques used both in medicine and in everyday life. Visual content is an example of one of the instruments of influence. It can be divided into two types: static and dynamic visual content. Each type has its own nature and the impact on the work of our perception organs and the analysis of environmental information. Various studies worldwide explore various kinds of visual content and its impacts on human beings.

The beneficial effects on the level of mental fatigue were proven for "restorative environments", such as natural landscapes [4]. Psychologists in relaxation therapy used audio content to accelerate the rehabilitation in cases of depression or reduce a general level of stress [5].

However, not only visual content that we observe in the natural environment can be used to improve the psycho-emotional state of a person. It is proven that the observation of a complex visual structure based on the self-similarity of elements (i.e. fractal images) activates the areas of the human brain responsible for relaxation and recovery processes, and also improves the functional state of the brain [6, 7]. This should take into account the characteristics responsible for the reproduction and quality of visual content. Images with a frame rate of 10 Hz activate the nerve endings of the brain better than blurred or Quick-images. [8]

The effects of the dynamic visual content used in the performances of the laser theater Lux Aeterna are similar to the techniques described above. A group of scientific researchers, who aimed at studying and analyzing the impact of visual content on the human condition created by using laser radiation, was created on the basis of ITMO University [9-11]. Previous experiments were conducted only using the pre- / post-test method, so we want to determine the effect for long-term use.

A new research study was conducted to assess the impact of sessions performed in the laser theater Lux Aeterna on a larger population sample, and regularly observe and evaluate the impact of the dynamic visual content generated by the theater on the psycho-emotional state of people.

[1] E-mail adress: matveev_nv@mail.ru , ikirill2193@gmail.com

2 Methods

2.1 Participants

In total, 70 students enrolled in the first year of the bachelor's degree at the ITMO University initially participated in the study; however, 30 participants (20 female and 10 male, aged 20 ± 3 years) were admitted to data processing due to the irregular participation in the group of participants. Each participant gave informed consent to participate in the study by filling out the form in accordance with ICH Harmonised Tripartite Guideline for GCP. To distribute the participants across equal groups, testing was conducted to determine the level of educational stress. Based on the data received, the participants were divided into two equally sized groups: the work group and the control group. The composition of the groups took into account the data on student achievement in the first semester of studies and the factors that potentially affect the level of learning stress among students (e.g. residence at the time of the experiment: with parents / in the dormitory / in the apartment (separately)), general emotional state, and subjective evaluation of a personal stress level.

2.2 Procedure

The premises of the laser theater Lux Aeterna operating on the basis of the ITMO University were selected as the site of the experiment, where the visual content was broadcasted. The theater is a spherical dome (planetarium) with the height of 6.3m and the diameter of 10m. The number of seats is 30. The dynamic visual content was generated using laser radiation (Kvant laser module / 3W / full color equipment). The results of recent studies, conducted in the dome of the laser theater, showed a positive effect of visual content on human performance and on brain function (states of altered consciousness [12], relaxation). In this regard, it was decided to assess the influence of visual content generated by laser radiation on the psycho-emotional state of a person. The dynamic visual content is projected on the screen placed under the spherical dome of the laser theater by passing the laser radiation through the liquid optical medium and optical elements arranged on a movable platform. As the laser is reflected and refracted in the optical media, the display content, consisting of complex shapes with a high degree of self-similarity, can be observed. To assess the degree of self-similarity, the fractal dimension of the image is used, which helps create unique (randomly generated) content and obtain visual images based on the optical characteristics and mathematical calculations. The obtained images projected on the spherical screen of the theater are similar to their natural analogs. They have smooth shapes and outlines that can be compared to the examples of a natural landscape or represented in the form of some kind of living organisms. Visual content with the elements of natural similarity does not cause discomfort to the viewer, as it is subconsciously perceived by her as a natural image. At the same time, the variable dynamic content is achieved by using various combinations of optical elements. The visual content session is accompanied by a calm audio composition.

During the experiment, the students in the work and control groups were required to pass a Bourdon test once every two weeks, a proof-of-effect test to assess the volume, concentration and sustainability of attention. The test is conducted by means of special forms with rows of random (Cyrillic alphabet) letters. The participant viewing the form row by row selects the letters indicated in the instruction by clicking computer mouse buttons. The test run time is 10 minutes; every 60 seconds the algorithm for selecting the character in the line is automatically changed. Thus, the participant of the test needs to monitor the correctness and the way of selecting the symbols. After all data measurements were made, the work group was proposed to assist a laser performance session of 20-25 min in the theater dome. This series of procedures, organized during the whole spring semester, was required for the participants to pass the test.

To determine the level of their educational stress, the students were asked to take the test based on the method of Yu.V.Scherbatyh. The testing was carried out at the beginning and in the end of the experiment. A psychological test included a set of questions divided into three parts: the contribution of individual factors to the overall state of stress (14 questions); the stress associated with the study (18 questions), and the stress management techniques (4 questions). Each part included several questions, assessing its response from 1 to 10 points. For the part with the multiple choice, it was required to note the choice made by the student, or make own choice if there was no suitable option. The total average score reflecting the overall level of participant's learning stress (from 1 to 10 points) was calculated based on the results of the answers obtained for three parts.

3 Results

At the end of the experiment, we obtained the output from the Bourdon test results and the Shcherbatykh test, helping determine the level of educational stress and academic performance of the participating students in the last two semesters. The results of the output parameters obtained from the Burdon test- the correctness factor and the productivity factor (PF) - were analyzed. The correctness factor was calculated as the ratio of the total volume of relatively correctly scanned symbols and erroneously (or missed) selected values. The PF was calculated as the multiplication of the correctness factor by the total number of scanned symbols. The dynamic changes in the mean values of the PFs calculated for the work group and the control group is shown in the graph below (Fig. 1). On both graphs, the confidence intervals are plotted for the PF values. The scores corresponding to the productivity factor are marked on the scale Y.

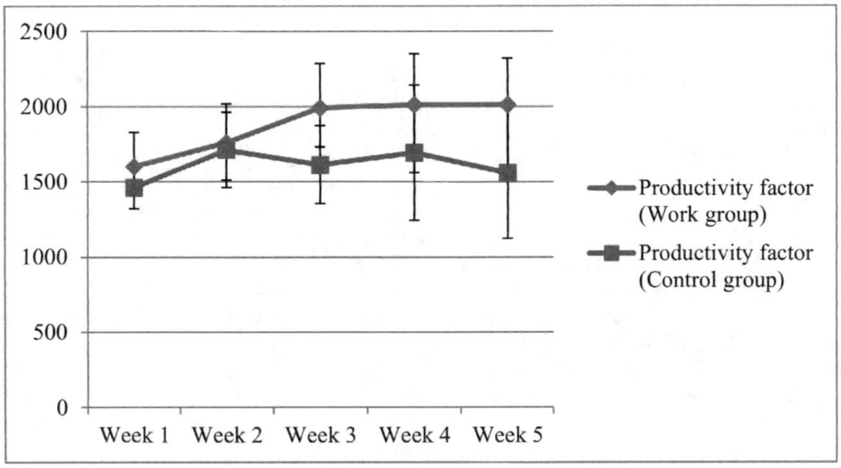

Fig. 1. The change in the productivity factor (mean value) during the experiment.

Having obtained the PF values, we analyzed two related data samples by calculating the Wilcoxon signed-rank test for the work and control groups in the beginning and at the end of the experiment. The criterion for Wilcoxon signed-ranks allows us to determine whether the change in the PF (and the passing of the Bourdon test as a whole) affects the viewing of visual content during the experiment. The Wilcoxon signed-rank test is intended to compare the values measured under two different conditions on the same sample of subjects. It allows us to establish not only the direction of changes but also their severity, that is, it is able to determine whether the shift in one direction is more intensive than in the other. The values for the first and the fifth week of the experiment were compared. In order to draw conclusions about the effectiveness of the impact of visual content on the test Bourdon results for the work and control groups, the statistical significance asymptotic value must be less than 0.05. Statistics Z shows the standard deviation of values between the first and the fifth week. Test statistic for the work group is $Z = 2{,}4$ (in absolute value); two-sided asymptotic significance of 0.016. For the control group test statistic is $Z = 0.7$; two-sided asymptotic significance 0.448. Since the asymptotic significance for the work group is less than 0.05, the Z statistics show that the presence of visual content effectively affects the stability of the productive passage of the Bourdon test and the improvement of the final totals. In the control group, the asymptotic significance is greater than 0.05, which means that in the absence of visual content during the experiment, the results of the Bourdon test do not have any significant changes at the beginning and end points of the study, or the lack of positive dynamics in the change in the parameter of the PF. Table 1 presents the results of statistical criteria for the Wilcoxon signed-rank test for all of the conducted methodologies (Table 1).

Table 1. Statistical criteria the Wilcoxon test according to test results

Statistical criteria / Tests	Work group			Control group		
	Δ mean (5 week-1week)	Z	Asymptotic significance	Δ mean (5 week-1week)	Z	Asymptotic significance
Bourdon test (PF points)	411	2.401	0.016	86.6	0.7	0.484
Shcherbatyh Test	-1.3	2.521	0.012	0.8	1.897	0.058

Academic progress	0.2	1.265	0.206	0.2	0.541	0.589

Based on the results of the Shcherbatyh learning stress test, we obtained several data samples with the values of the general level of learning stress in the subjects at the time of the experiment and after its completion. The analysis of the test results of the work group showed a significant reduction in the level of learning stress in 80% of the group (a decrease of -1.3 by 0.3 – 1.3 points). This indicator did not change in 15%, and in 5% of the work group, the level of learning stress increased (an increase of -1.3 by 0.1-0.4 points). After calculating the Wilcoxon signed-rank criterion for the values of the learning stress level (before and after the experiment), the values of Z = 2.521 and the asymptotic significance (bilateral) of 0.012 were obtained. Due to the fact that the asymptotic significance is less than 0.05, the data can be considered reliable, and the Z statistics indicate a significant change in the level of learning stress. In the case of the control group, the results showed that 66% of the subjects had an increase in the level of total stress (an increase of 0.8 by 1 – 3.3 points), 30% of participants decreased their level of total stress (a decrease of 0.8 by 0.1-0.7 points), and for 4%,it remained unchanged. In the calculation of the criterion for the signed-ranks of Wilcoxon, the values Z = 1.897 and the asymptotic significance of 0.058 were obtained. The last indicator is more than 0.05, which means that the control group changes in the level of learning stress are insignificant and depend exclusively on the subjective characteristics of the subjects in the control group.

In conclusion, the analysis of the results of academic progress among the students of the work and control groups, namely the assessments for two semesters in the exact disciplines (physics, mathematics) were carried out. The exact disciplines were chosen as a factor for analysis, as these disciplines require increased concentration of attention during the students' learning process. The results of the average score for the six months in these disciplines did not show any significant change. After calculating the criterion for Wilcoxon's signed-ranks, we obtained the following statistics: for the work group, Z = 1.265 and asymptotic significance 0.206; in the control group, Z = 0.541 and asymptotic significance 0.589. The asymptotic significance indicators are greater than 0.05 in both groups, which points to either a slight change in the academic progress in the exact disciplines or to a complete absence of such changes.

4 Discussion

The research was aimed at assessing the impact of dynamic audiovisual content on a person's psychoemotional state, subject to regular visits to sessions based on the performances of the laser theater Lux Aeterna. To this end, three sets of data were tested: the productivity and sustainability of attention, the general level of learning stress and academic progress of students. Based on the results obtained, it can be concluded that regular attendance of audiovisual content sessions using the laser theater Lux Aeterna can have a positive impact on productivity and concentration of attention in the performance of monotonous work (with the presence of emotional and intellectual load) or help maintain stable results in the performance of learner. Also, the regular exposure to dynamic audiovisual content can significantly reduce the level of learning stress. The research showed a decrease in the level of learning stress by more than three points from the initial level among 80% of the subjects. In addition, at the end of the test, a survey was conducted among those for whom the test shows a decrease in the level of stress, and in 60% of cases, the results of self-reported confirmed the results of the Shcherbatykh test. Correlations between the level of learning stress and academic progress were not found. Thus, it can be argued that there is no influence of dynamic audiovisual content on the student's progress and this parameter depends only on the subjective features of each participant in the experiment.

In this regard, the use of dynamic audio-visual content sessions based on the laser theater Lux Aeterna can be considered as an alternative relaxation method that allows changing the level of learning stress in people, increasing productivity in the performance of monotonous work and improving general well-being. The key factor for obtaining a positive result will be the regular use of this technique in the long term.

The researched content can be offered in specially allocated restorative rooms. However, the specific features of working with the visual image of the Lux Aeterna theater can be applied when creating general lighting in working and home environments. Studying the dynamic ranges of brightness and radiation spectrum variation can help identify the patterns that positively influence the psychoemotional state of a person, and transfer them to the operating modes of the common lighting systems.

References

1. Ioffe K.I. "Biological influence of visible light on the human body." *International Scientific and Technical Journal "Lighting Engineering and Power Engineering*. No. 3 (2008): 21-29.
2. Ovchinnikov S.S. and Serobaba A.A. "Evaluation of the effectiveness of the influence of the light environment on the human body." *Lighting and electric power industry.* No. 4 (2008): 4-10.
3. Zakgeim, Alexander L. "Light-emitting Diode Illumination Systems: Energy Efficiency, Visual Perception, and Safety for Health." *Light & engineering* 21.2 (2013).
4. Berto, Rita. "Exposure to restorative environments helps restore attentional capacity." *Journal of environmental psychology* 25.3 (2005): 249-259.
5. Beck, Bolette Daniels, Åse Marie Hansen, and Christian Gold. "Coping with work-related stress through Guided Imagery and Music (GIM): Randomized controlled trial." *Journal of music therapy* 52.3 (2015): 323-352.
6. Tkacheva, L. O. "Effects of fractal dynamic images on human functional state." *Vestnik Saint-Petersburg University (RUS)*. 12.2 (2010).
7. Tkacheva, L. O., I. A. Gorbunov, and A. D. Nasledov. "Reorganization of system brain activity while understanding visually presented texts with the increasing completeness of information." *Human Physiology* 41.1 (2015): 11-21.
8. Bakardjian, Hovagim, Toshihisa Tanaka, and Andrzej Cichocki. "Emotional faces boost up steady-state visual responsesforbrain–computer interface." *Neuroreport* 22.3 (2011): 121-125.
9. Matveev N., Prokopenko V., Sapunova N., Fridman D., Research into the influence of light-music performances on psychophysiological states, Light & Engineering - 2016, Vol. 24, No. 2, pp. 22-24.
10. Matveev N., Shcheglov S., Romanova G., Koneva T., Modeling of the laser device for the stress therapy// Proceedings of SPIE - 2017, Vol. 10239, pp. 102390H
11. Morgia S. Wellness keeps aging workforce young. Benefits and pensions monitor, 2014, 24, pp 36–37.
12. Ludwig A. "Altered states of consciousness" *Archives of general psychiatry*. — N 15, 1966. P. 225—234.

Architectural lighting in search of identity: The environmental approach

Marina Sokolova[1] *, and *Marina* Silkina [1*]

[1]Moscow Institute of Architecture (State Academy), Department of Design of Architectural Environment, 107031, Rozhdestvenka St., 11/4, building. 1, p. 4, Moscow, Russia

Abstract. This article examines the perception of architectural environment, and various approaches and methods of its light organization, including the design of evening illumination and objects of light design. Traced influence of the figurative discoveries of light art on light design, and the problems of the formation of individual light-plastic code of the urban environment as a means of manifesting the identity of the place are revealed.

Today, at the era of globalization, the disappearance of cultural and national differences, the problems of preserving identity come to the fore in many areas of an architectural project, and, most notably, in the design of the urban environment. Studies of visual perception of the environment, and awareness of environmental identity started in the 1960s with the work of American planner Kevin Lynch "The Image of the City" [1]. Today, the relevance of this problem is becoming all the more important.

The interest in the urban environment and the emergence of ideas for meaningful design of urban space were a "postmodern" reaction to the global paradigm of modernism - functionalism that took dominant positions in the world architecture of the 1960s. The transition from modernism to postmodernism, from the lapidary nature of geometry to plastic complexity and organic, from the abstract form to the style quotation and contextuality, is a movement between the so-called "strong" and "weak" project orientations determined by the different type of relationship between the designer and the world (G. Courierova) [2, c. 60]. A "strong" installation is the purity and clarity of regular geometric composite construction, confirmed by the discoveries of modernism. The method of organic design, characteristic for the "weak" design setting, is directly opposite, thus emphatically concrete, reflexive, and historical. It is a direct-sensual experience of the flow of time. "Only by freeing ourselves of all abstractions, can we truly enter the living stream of experience, and expertly realize ... the concrete image of the world and life in its continuous formation and transformation" (cf. on 2, c. 77]. The postmodern design model is distinguished by the multidimensionality of values, leading to unpredictable innovation in plastic solutions [3].

The problems of complexity and multilayered spatial and temporal development of the urban environment, the treatment to the person, their relationship with architecture and space, the problems of contextual design and the need for changes formulated by Kevin Lynch

* Corresponding author: eremych@inbox.ru, marina.a.silkina@gmail.com

(1960) [1] and Jane Jacobs (1961) [4] were further developed in the works of Christopher Alexander (1977) [5], Herman Hertzberger (1991) [6], etc. Ideas originated in the West were quickly picked up in the 1980s by progressive Russian architects. In particular, Alexei Gutnov, Vyacheslav Glazychev, theoreticians Andrey Ikonnikov, Alexander Rappaport, Oleg Genisaretsky, Georgy Minervin and others, who changed in many respects the ideas of Russian designers about methods of working with urban environment, have developed a new method - the environmental approach.

Russian domestic researchers in the "general field" of the project culture have defined the fundamental difference between the concepts of "environmental space" and "architecture." In contrast with an architectural object with its completeness, static, invariability, the environment is characterized by such qualities as mobility, dynamism, disconnection, openness, and incompleteness. It is interpreted as a material, volatile subject-spatial interaction. The core of a design model of environment is the "metabolism" of people's interaction in specific conditions. The created "figurative construct," including architectural means, is calculated in advance as changing in time with "open", i.e., uncertain and indefinite, future. Unlike the architectural construct, the description of the environment is built during architectural practice solely by verbal means. (V. Glazychev) [3,7,8].

Analysis of the properties of architecture and environment indicates their relation to fundamentally different languages of culture, and two different types of cognitive mechanisms - analytical and sensory, which points to the need for their interconnected developmental dominance. Differences lie in the field of the psychology of perception, the type of reaction of the consumer. In environmental design, the environment is not only the environment of something (or somebody) or a combination of elements or conditions, among which an object or a person. First of all, it is the interconnectedness and interpenetration of the components of the environment that affect its characteristics (V. Glazychev) [3,7,8].

The relationship between environmental design and "easel" art is determined by an artistically oriented vision of project tasks. Like the painter the environmental designer tends to create not so much a building and its subject filling as its environmental state, the "atmosphere" that determines the imaginative beginning. The mediocre approach in design reveals the inter-permeability of types of artistic activity boundaries whose object of interest is the environment space. The mediocre approach, with its synthesizing "need to delve into everything" (V. Glazychev) [3,7,8], ensures "the cultural integrity of modern civilization" (G. Courierova) [3, 9,10].

If the term architectural "space" is disclosed as a continuum-pure duration and voidness, the term environmental space is understood as a particular case of space – an extended non-uniform materialized beginning where integrity is primary and dominates over dissection. The environmental space acts as a collection of space and material filling. It is characterized by priority of cohesion, leakage, and viscosity. The environmental space is a system of spiritual senses and material conditions contributing the dominance of the emotional principle over the rational, the synthetic over the analytic (I. Smekalov) [11].

The problems of professional relations with the environment are in the plane of the perception and interaction with the user. Physically, the architectural space is formed by what it is surrounded by, or by objects within it and visible in the light. And although we cannot explain by words what makes space particularly expressive, it can be determined by the height and perspective, giving a feeling of fullness without stiffness, an equilibrium between capacity and openness, and the combination of all kinds of factors, such as illumination, acoustics, a special ambience, people and, finally, the user's own mood, that affect the perception of space and emotion. "Architecture is a phenomenological discipline, which can be understood only at the moment when people move through the architectural space. If you turn your head, take a look, or turn the other way, you will see different space. You have had this opportunity to experience the space only because you have made a move. Also you will notice another texture of the surfaces and feel other materiality of the building depends on your move. Observation and analysis during (and after) these simple changes in one's position are the only way for true understanding and feeling of architecture. Referring to the book, "with even the greatest in the world of construction illustrations, you cannot understand what this building really is. Without being near it, you will not hear the melody that arises from its special acoustics, you will not feel its materiality and spatial energy, its unique play of light." (S. Holl) [cf. 12].

Studies of the integrity of visual perception, visual field, synthesis and differentiation of attention, problems of visual thinking and visualization revealed a similar device of instrumental-conceptual apparatus of medium and easel creativity (V.Rozin) [13]. Since the architectural environment is not only an object of functional use, but also an object of sensory experience, it must be created not only on the basis of technical calculations but, first of all, taking into account the aspects of perception and "empathy", formed by means of artistic expressiveness, or figurative language. For the first time in relation to architecture the notion of "language" was introduced by Charles Jenks in his book The Language of the Architecture of Postmodernism [3, 14].

Kevin Lynch proposed conscious designing of "image" of public spaces, combining psychology and sociology with urban planning and architecture. For him, primary was the problem of perception of urban environment by man, its comprehension and comfortable orientation among it – the formation of clear, readable and at the same time unique images represented by universal elements revealed in the general structure of the city: paths, borders, areas, nodes, [1]. Rethinking the problems of town planning Alexei Gutnov formulated more general terms that define the structure of spatial organization: "frame", "fabric", "plasma". He paid special attention to changing subject content of the urban environment with design objects – including urban furniture, navigation and lighting systems [15]. And if the "fabric" basically determines the areas, forms the boundaries, contains the dominants (the landmarks), and the "skeleton" basically forms the paths and nodes, the "plasma" creates elusive combination of objects and spaces into single environmental integrity.

In darkness, the illumination undoubtedly plays a dominant role in shaping the image of the urban environment perceived by the inhabitants. The environment perception is offered through the "flashing" of individual objects (architectural lighting) and the "manifestation" of the entire structure (functional lighting). "Background" lighting is of great importance (e.g. windows' light in buildings). Functional lighting is subordinated to the existing road and transport structure and does not create anything in itself, but architectural, landscape and information lighting shapes the unique environment that a person perceives, and by means of which, the "image of the city" which is formed in his consciousness as the carrier-reflection of his identity [16].

Unfortunately, today there is a dangerous trend of unification in the design of urban lighting, including systems of light navigation. Many lighting and navigation projects for large cities differ little from the point of view of the formation of the environmental state and the appearance of the objects. Such a light environment does not aim to identify, preserve, manifest, exacerbate or form a new identity conditioned by the environmental context. It is unlikely that this return to unification and globalization can be justified by the need to ensure a universal reading of the spatial arrangement and orientation information. Universalism leads to emotional "deafness," the loss of environmental historical memory, the most fragile component of urban fabric. Ideas to start a project from scratch are absurd and disastrous, since under the pretext of having to start from the beginning, existing buildings are being destroyed and the empty space is filled with practically "sterile" structures. The different meanings of everything that has taken place are similar to the old layers of paint lying one over the other. In their entirety, they form a primer for us to know where a new layer can be placed, a new meaning that will change the whole a little. This process is an evolutionary process of transformation, whereby the obsolete meanings become the background for the creation of a new one. With the help of such a dialectical process, a continuous thread between the past and the future is preserved, and the connection of times is realized (H. Hertzberger) [17]. Of course, the content that is brought into the urban environment today should not be excessively individual or active, but it must nevertheless take into account the environmental context, respond to it, solve the problems of manifesting the nature of the environment, and be the bearer of a special "spirit of place".

Through a special spatial character and a system of landmarks, and through a certain essence, an intangible substance called the "spirit of the place" is cultivated, in accordance with which our ancestors' lives proceeded, and the way they perceived their habitat. In today's economic and cultural globalization the problem of the loss of identity is becoming especially urgent, but there are the differences between places and cities that give them special value, thus provoking us to move through spaces – to travel. In addition to orienting in space, it is important for people to identify themselves with a certain place, the features of which that are manifested by their spatial arrangement and a set of characteristic plastic qualities. The object-spatial relations perceived during the day and in the dark are replaced by light ones which can echo the existing architectural structures, and create another composite picture. Architectural lighting, contributing to the formation of the "night image of the city" and orientation in it, is most relevant for the historic city center. Highlighting monuments of architecture suggests the perception of the night city as a more articulated, aggravated image of the city of the day, where historical features become dominant environmental reference points. Cities are associated, as a rule, with their signature architectural objects, though the means for creating their evening image differ little: in Paris the Eiffel Tower is lit, in Moscow the Kremlin, and in St. Petersburg the Peter and Paul Fortress. These are the image objects with which we actually identify cities. The methods of such architectural "flashing" are also almost always uniform. Thus, evening lighting only shows the existing architectural and town-planning features of the city.

Where is the inspiration for new solutions? Undoubtedly, in the historical context, landscape, planning structure, national and regional cultural and plastic tradition, color preferences, from which new solutions must grow, form a certain composite and imaginative integrity, and thus new landmarks and bearing features of the environment identity. Among the most characteristic examples of the designer's interaction with the components of the environmental identity we can mention Paris where the signs addressed are turned into objects of souvenirs, as well as the recognizable signs on the houses in Rome, and the sign of the metro in London. So the element of the orientation system goes beyond its function and environmental visual image, and becomes an object identified with the city, its non-architectural symbol, which has a relationship to the brand of the city and the formation of identity in the fashionable branding of territories today.

While designing a light design solution it is important to set tasks not to create a universal, often contradictory new environment structure, but to show or adjust the existing urban environment through the light layer using non-standard and even radical design solutions. An example is the light memorial on the site of the destroyed towers of the World Trade Center (Twin Towers) in New York. Of course, this is not the creation of a new identity, it is a manifestation of the "spirit of place" through a light "architecture" – installation. A similar solution showing the lost is Roger Narboni's project for São Paulo (Brazil), where the light master plan for the entire city is built on the manifestation of the historical landscape and the invisible rivers of the Spirits. So in Moscow it is possible to "restore" the walls of the White

City, and on Neglinka Street and Kuznetsky Most Street, to "return" Trubnaya Square to the image of a light river - Neglinnuyu, hidden underground in the early 19th century.

Perception is the ability to release (extract) certain aspects from context to place them in a new context. Each new idea begins with observing things differently. Observing the architecture of other times or places, it is necessary to direct our eyes from the objects to the place which create the form, to look through the definiteness of the form revealing the essence of the place and thus shifting the accent from the architecture to what the environment is, and to discover its influence on the succession of generations and cultures. Although we do not control our impressions, we can, at least, develop our eyes, gaining the habit of fixing things on paper. Among all the possibilities of reproducing the subject, the drawing is the most consistent with this goal, and is more effective than, for example, photographs that everyone takes from time to time. In many cases, photography is the most appropriate means to present the situation objectively. However, the dignity of the picture is that, looking at things with greater accuracy and, above all, becoming more rigorous to what seems important, the severity in fixation will increase. It then becomes possible, having got rid of unnecessary details, to fix the very essence, and the formula of the object. The only accessible way out of our own limitations is the development of figurative thinking, the connection to the riches of collective memory. Turning back to fundamental, which is unaltered components, we discover the existence of common features – archetypes in various objects. And thus we find the "cross-section of everything" – an unchanging element at the base of all examples that always recalls memories, can be the starting point form. Today the means of the whole array of the past are endless. Elements freed from specific time frames have more general meaning and appear in different guises, obviously because they can be related to basic human values that are preserved, albeit with varying emphasis and in different style languages preserving the basic generative grammar (H. Herzberger) [17].

How can you analyze the environment? Architectural forms and their location in space can be likened to composition of their primary elements. In this abstract figure, with the help of the semantic component of the elements themselves, those invisible characteristics of the place, its spirit, which predetermined the location of large and small architectural forms in space and the growth in it of objects of the natural landscape, are concentrated. To sum up, this drawing can be called a plastic equivalent of the place visualized by means of light technologies in the dark.

Examples of growing an environmental solution from the context can be seen in a number of architectural projects today, for example, the project of the Cultural Center for Santiago de Compostela, created by the architect Peter Eisenman. As Eisenmann himself says, he always tried to grow his buildings from the ground, so that they would form a single whole without breaking the connection with it. The idea of layering various tracks found on the site, not only visual, but also historical, symbolic, abstract, hypothetical and so on, has been developed by Eisenman long ago and consistently. The architect was influenced greatly by French philosopher Jacques Derrida, author of the theory of deconstruction, denying the existence of an absolute beginning and arguing that any beginning is preceded by a trace or a wreath of traces. Derrida argued: "There is nothing that would exist before anything else. There is no one truth. There is no absolute beginning. Everything opened before the tracks had begun. Before there was something, there had been a trace of something. Before there was something, this something had not been. Absence always precedes presence, because there would be no presence if there was not originally absence "[18, 19].

Eisenman's team identified four such tracks on the site: the topography of the hill on the construction site assigned to the new complex; a network of streets of the historic center of Santiago de Compostela; an abstract Cartesian network and a symbolic sign of the city - a shell of a shellfish. Then all these unrelated tracks were combined into a complex plexus to create an imaginary site that eventually became real. In other words, the beginning of the project was not a physical site allocated for construction, but traces, according to Derrida's theory and Eisenman's interpretations, found on this site and around. It is interesting to note that the intriguing tectonic form arose independently of the planned functions of the complex in the process of the artistic combination of abstract trace diagrams into a single sculptural landscape-environmental formation. The cast of plastic solution was a three-dimensional wooden layout, which inspired the customer to implement this particular design intent [18, 19].

Eisenman believes that a person in the architectural space perceives its organization and its device by his mind, and the vague sensations of the space by the senses. Describing the features of his own creative process, Eisenman calls geological, topological, social, economic, technical diagrams taken from the plot and forming project layers that form the structure and body of the building, such as its spelling, morphology and syntax, and what eventually becomes an architectural space, poetry born from heart. Where the mind ends and the heart begins is almost impossible to be determined. However, the traces of these diagrams, "organized by reason", in the inner space of the complex – the inclusion of a dark stone in the floor, the relief drops of the fragments of the ceiling – are perceived precisely by heart and, more likely, even by artistic feeling, as a single multilayered spatial composition [18, 19].

Another architect, Steven Holl, also believes that it is necessary to create a new one by imposing simple components on each other. Components can be a function, a form, a social aspect, a historical fact, a natural or social phenomenon. Holl's architecture is distinguished by the project translation of these semantic components into an artistic and plastic invention – the geometric form, the principle of compositional division, and the use of material and color. The materialization of the architectural idea at the stage of sketching in a mock-up or drawing with elements of painting translates it into an artistic technology, which leads to a clearly read design of the architectural structure, and transparency of the means used. As a result, the pleasure of the viewer in easily guessing the plastic form responses to the context or function assignments. "I believe that architecture needs to be a continuation of the place, and it needs to meet the goals that it is laid down. My first book, "Anchoring," explains the relationship of the structure to the place in which it is located, with its culture and metaphysical principles. If the author's architectural concept ... can penetrate deeper into the cultural and spiritual aura of the place, then it enriches it with a new cultural significance, individual and modern ... It is important to hook on the idea that hovers in the air of each place. It can be anything: stories passed from mouth to mouth, living folklore, inimitable humor "(S. Holl) [op. 12].

Is it possible to use this method in the design of night lighting? This design does not exist in isolation from the general cultural field. It always follows the discoveries, whether they are the discoveries in the field of art or scientific and technical innovations. It admits everything that can affect the form and function, but it is the form that determines our visual perception of the objective world. In the field of light design, the choice of certain means of expressiveness is not accidental, but largely formed under the influence of artists and sculptors who began to work with light as a means of creating an artistic work – "light sculpture", when light does not illuminate an object, but becomes an "object" itself.

If in the early 20th century light was used more as a source – artists were more concerned with shadows, and reflection effects (Marcel Duchamp, László Moholy-Nagy), then in the 1960s the source itself. Even later the light itself becomes an object of art, which was due to the emergence of new technologies, in particular the wide use of neon, light projections. The artistic means created contribute to the compositional organization of the environment in modern urban design, turning not only individual small forms but also large urban spaces into art objects. This was promoted by such masters as Lucio Fontana, Dan Flavin, Francois Moreliet, James Turrell, Bruce Nauman, and contemporary artists such as Massimo Uberti, Carlo Bernardini, Björn Dahlem, and Jim Sanborn et al.

Unlike other types of art, abstract plastic arts, including design of the light environment, convey sensory images through the associative possibilities of means of expressiveness – the types of composite connections, color-inverse relations, the configuration of lines, and forms of rhythm, etc. As examples of modern urban design show, solutions directly related to the language of art, which are successive to artistic discoveries of the 20th and 21st centuries, are able to successfully interact with the subject but spatial environment, complementing it organically. Small architectural forms, equipment elements, navigation systems, can become art objects, like city sculpture creating a memorable visual image of the environmental fragment (street, quay, square, etc.) both in the light and in the dark.

The use of light as an independent composite tool are traced in the modern design of urban equipment and elements of improvement. The urban environment easily "admits" these point-like, accenting, contrasting light-color solutions that do not require consistency with all other components of the light environment, and functional and architectural lighting. The compositional structure of such decisions, as a rule, is determined by the plasticity of the elements of urban design themselves. It emphasizes and manifests such plasticity and has a distinct light structure, which creates prerequisites for the development of the identity of the territories and the formation of their visual image in the dark.

The connection between light art and modern lighting solutions can be found in the concept of the light "gateway" for Paris – the "Paris Crown" Lighting Master Plan (France) by the French lighting designer Roger Narboni. This approach is also illustrated by lighting solutions for Finsbury Avenue Square in London (United Kingdom) and Plaza del Torico in Teruel Teruel (Spain), where the lines, in the first case, structure space, and, in the second, introduce free dynamics of light "strokes". Other examples of “light strokes” are a solution of light guides embedded in the pavement, lawns and benches of the University Entrance Square of the Ben-Gurion University of the Negev in Beer-Sheva, Israel; a solution of light lines located at a slight angle to each other, resting in the High Line Park in New York, USA; and a dynamic broken line running along the ends of the seating facility that organizes the public space in Hamburg, Germany.

Using plastic language, it is possible to find a picture of environmental identity for each fragment of a city or the city as a whole. Growing up from different historical and geographical circumstances, the cities have a unique pattern of planning fabric and a special character. Just to name a few examples: the two high banks of Prague, connected by "lacing bridges"; the clinging to the water "sink" of Amsterdam; spreading "ice floes" of the islands of Stockholm united by the structure of streets; and the "cuttings" of Osman that cut through the "goat trails" of Paris.

What can we say about Moscow in this connection? At the level of the general plan, the color is working – there is the red triangle of the Kremlin in the center; the green ring of the Boulevard Ring; and the multi-colored ring of Sadovaya streets. Bypassing the triangle, the ring crosses the blue snake of the Moscow River, creating an eye-orienting road. The next layer of the city structure is the rays that organize the city fabric.

Let us now turn to what can be called the deep characteristics of Moscow as the ancient capital. The so-called "Russian spirit" in Moscow consists of simplicity and geometry of white stone construction, wooden architecture, architecture of classicism, constructivism of the 1920s, monumentality of the mid-20th century, and the rapidly developed new quarters. In the basis are the pattern and the constructor. On top of that is the general characteristic of Moscow at all times, which is "merchant decoration" (decor, details), brightness, bustle, fairness, as well as a constant desire to break the composition of the foreign object. All these lead to a common collage of the environment. Thus, in the course of development, a high-rise tower or any other construction of a different style may appear, set obliquely, non-scale, and foreign in the city. And in some cases, constant changes in the terrain lead to a combination in the environment with fragments of completely unrelated stylistics, scales, heights, and geometries. Thus, a kind of environment "out of nothing."

Translating previous reflections into the language of abstract forms, one can obtain a whole series of light solutions, using the general light-plastic code of the place, i.e. "structure and collage". This helps to create a systematically organized light frame of a certain place, in which other elements – complex, dynamic, multicolored, and organically-smooth, can be found. In another situation, the initial complexity, contrast, collage of the medium can lead to a contrasting connection of the fragments of the light solution, thus a string of different compositions combined by some limiting principle (number, size, height of the light pattern).

Why is it so expressively effective that there can be plastic and compositionally clear light accents in the environment of a modern city? In the situation of "visual noise", which exists in most cases as a result of spontaneous human actions at different times, they create a certain frame of perception of space in the evening and structure space. They are most noticeable in chaos because they are extremely contrasting with the environment.

Is it expedient to find another way? Is it really necessary to give light the ability to form a new identity, both for local urban spaces and cities as a whole so as to create urban spaces where a unique light solution itself becomes an "environmental magnet"? Is there a danger that such a radical use of lighting will destroy the existing architectural spaces? Can light being used not only as a means of illumination, but also as an independent component of the environment, as a light object, sculpture, architecture, space, be self-sufficient? Should light solutions follow the device of the environment, respond to it or be opposed to it? Can these decisions be made randomly? Will this help the formation of new images with quality and comfort of orientation in space? One thing is clear: interest in such radical decisions is much in focus today. Therefore, an experiment and development of new design principles for the light organization of the urban environment, which grow out of context but do not deny the possibility of creating a new identity and environmental magnets in the evening city environment, is necessary. How is it possible to create a design solution as put in the words of the architect Peter Eisenman: "To be there, to walk there –- it makes you be amazed" [19].

Designing a light-plastic space is a special creative task. Attention to the peculiarities of a particular place, to its landscape, cultural-historical, social and other contexts, to its "spirit" requires a light designer to be particularly sensitive. An individual approach to light design becomes a necessary condition today for preserving the unique face of each place and each city.

References

1. K. Lynch, *The Image of the City* (The MIT Press, 1960)
2. G.G. Kurerova, *Italyanskaya model dizayna [Italian Design Model]* (Biblioteka dizaynera. Seriya Zarubezhnyiy dizayn, Fotopoligraficheskiy tsentr VNIITE, Moscow, 1993)
3. M. A. Sokolova, *Sovremennyiy plasticheskiy yazyik v obuchenii arhitektora-dizaynera: Uchebnoe posobie* [*Modern plastic language in the training of the architect-designer: Textbook*] (Arhitektura-S, Moscow, 2016)
4. J. Jacobs, *The Death and Life of Great American Cities* (Random House, New York, 1961)
5. C. Alexander, *A Pattern Language: Towns, Buildings, Construction* (Oxford University Press, USA. 1977)

6. H. Hertzberger, *Lessons for Students in Architecture* (NAi010 Publishers, Rotterdam, 1991, 2005)
7. V.L. Glazyichev, *Yazyik i metod hudozhestvennogo proektirovaniya [Language and method of artistic design],* Dekorativnoe iskusstvo, **11** (1973)
8. V.L. Glazyichev *Sotsialno-ekologicheskaya interpretatsiya gorodskoy sredyi [Socio-ecological interpretation of the urban environment]* (Nauka, Moscow, 1984)
9. G.G. Kurerova *Ekologicheskaya orientatsiya v sovremennoy proektnoy kulture Zapadnoy Evropyi // Sotsialno-kulturnyie problemyi obraza zhizni i predmetnoy sredyi [Ecological orientation in the modern project culture of Western Europe // Socio-cultural problems of the way of life and the subject environment]* Trudyi VNIITE, Tehnicheskaya estetika, Vol. **52**, p. 85 (1987)
10. G.G. Kurerova *Proektnaya kontseptualistika 80-h godov: novoe myishlenie i «inoe» myishlenie // Tvorcheskie napravleniya v sovremennom zarubezhnom dizayne [Project conceptualism of the 80s: new thinking and "other" thinking // Creative trends in contemporary foreign design]*, Trudyi VNIITE, Tehnicheskaya estetika, Vol. **60**, pp. 22-44 (1990)
11. I.V. Smekalov *Rol zhivopisi v proektnoy kulture sredovogo dizayna*: *Avtoref. dis. kand. iskusstv*.: 17.00.06 [The role of painting in the project culture of environmental design: Author's abstract. dis. Cand. Arts: 17.00.06] pp. 22-44 (VNIITE, Moscow, 2009)
12. S. Holl, zdes i dalee tsit. po: Nevlyutov M. Prakticheskaya fenomenologiya Stivena Holla [Here and below. by: Nevlyutov M. Practical phenomenology of Steven Holl] from https://archi.ru/world/66898/prakticheskaya-fenomenologiya-stivena-holla
13. V.M. Rozin, *Vizualnaya kultura i vospriyatie (Kak chelovek vidit i vosprinimaet mir)* [Visual culture and perception (How a person sees and perceives the world)] (Editorial URSS, Moscow, 1996).
14. M. A. Sokolova, *Modern visual language and plastic education*, AMIT **4 (13)** from http://www.marhi.ru/eng/AMIT/2010/4kvart10/sokolova/abstract.php (2010)
15. A.E. Gutnov, *Evolyutsiya gradostroitelstva* [The Evolution of Urban Planning] (Stroyizdat, Moscow, 1984)
16. M.A. Silkina, *Light reference points in a night city environment*//Light & Engineering. Vol. **23**, No. 2, pp. 29-33 (2015)
17. H. Hertzberger, *Space and the Architect: Lessons for Students in Architecture 2,* (010 Publishers. Rotterdam, 2000)
18. V. Belogolovskiy *V krasote li schaste? Beseda s Piterom Ayzenmanom [In beauty is happiness? Conversation with Peter Eisenman]*, Arhitekturnyiy Vestnik, **5** (2009)
19. P. Eisenman. *Lektsiya Pozdniy stil [Lecture Late Style]* 29.05. 2010. TsDH. Vyistavka ArhMoskva (2010)

Fractal analysis of the relationship between the visual complexity of laser show pictures and a human psychophysiological state

Nikolai Matveev[1], *Aleksandra* Sherstobitova[2], and *Olga* Gerasimova[1]

[1] Department of "The Higher School of Lighting Design", Saint Petersburg National Research University of Information Technologies, Mechanics and Optics (ITMO University), Saint-Petersburg, Russia

[2] Department of Light Technologies and Optoelectronics, Saint Petersburg National Research University of Information Technologies, Mechanics and Optics (ITMO University), Saint-Petersburg, Russia

Abstract. This paper presents the results of the fractal analysis of the relationship between the visual complexity of laser show pictures and its human aesthetic perception. Recommendations on the use of laser effects in the art therapy are presented

Keywords: psychophysiology, laser graphics, fractal dimension

1 Introduction

Today, many people are exposed to stress and its negative impact. In this respect, there is a need to correct a human psychophysiological state (and not only by medical means). The application of different audiovisual systems (Theta Mind's Eye, 2016; Mind Machines, 2016) can significantly improve people's quality of life. These systems can stimulate physiological and emotional activity of humans. Not only they have a relaxing effect, but also help people reduce anxiety and boost their productivity.

Some systems use flashes of light and rhythmic tones to affect the brain. Modern devices based on this principle consist of LED (light-emitting diode) glasses. The visual content of audiovisual systems includes pictures of nature or abstract images. The latter can be created by hand or generated by program code (Mental Rhythm, 2016). Fractal algorithms are often used to generate abstract graphics.

The term "fractal" was first introduced by B. Mandelbrot. It refers to a specific geometrical structure which has a property of self-similarity. Such objects can often be found in nature (trees, circulatory system, etc.) (Forsythe et al., 2011; Bourke, 2016). Today, fractal theory and fractal methods are used in engineering, medicine, art, and other fields. The fractal dimension D is the basic parameter for quantitative analysis of fractal forms. The Hausdorff dimension and the box dimension are mostly used in experimental science. The latter is defined by:

$$D = -\lim_{\varepsilon \to 0} \frac{\log N(\varepsilon)}{\log \varepsilon} \quad (1)$$

where $N(\varepsilon)$ is the minimum number of "balls" of radius ε required to cover a certain set (Crownover, 1995).

Today, the fractal dimension is a qualitative aesthetic measure of the visual complexity of paintings and artworks (Forsythe et al., 2011; Mureika, 2005; Taylor et al., 2007; Abbott, 2017). R. P. Taylor, A. Micolich, D. Jonas and other researchers discovered fractal structures in abstract paintings and found the relationship between the fractal dimension of artworks and their human visual perception (Taylor et al., 2001). Thus, paintings with the 1.3-1.5 fractal dimension were aesthetically more preferable to observers than the ones in the fractal dimension of 1.1-1.2 and 1.6-1.9. R. Taylor has also demonstrated beneficial effects of fractal forms on a human psychophysiological state (Forsythe et al., 2011; Taylor et al., 2001).

Laser projection systems gain popularity due to specific characteristics of laser radiation (monochromaticity, coherence, brightness, etc.). They are widely used in the entertainment industry and audiovisual art. These systems enable technicians to create various visual effects. The positive effects of laser projection relaxation methods were previously described by N. Matveev (Matveev, 2016). This paper presents a fractal analysis of the visual complexity of laser show pictures and their impact on human emotional state.

Fractal methods have been used for the quantitative and qualitative analysis of paintings for a long time (Forsythe et al., 2011; Mureika, 2005; Taylor et al., 2007; Abbott, 2017; Taylor et al., 2001). In this paper, we present the results of the original study on the use of laser show pictures.

2 Method

Several types of laser effects are used in light shows: lumia, beam and screen effects. For lumia effects, the laser beam passing through heterogeneous media creates different abstract shapes (interference patterns). To produce beam effects, technicians use smoke or dust and control the laser beam with mirrors, diffraction gratings, etc. For screen effects, laser graphics, texts and animated images are drawn by the laser beam on the projection surface (Daukantas, 2010).

We made pictures of different laser effects used in "Lux Aeterna Theatre" (Russia, Saint-Petersburg) (Lux Aeterna Theatre, 2017). These effects were created by laser technicians using Pangolin software (Pangolin Laser Systems, 2017). We selected 45 images that are most relevant for the purposes of our experiment and divided them into 3 sets of 15 images, where each set represented the corresponding laser effect. Laser show pictures are shown in Figure 1.

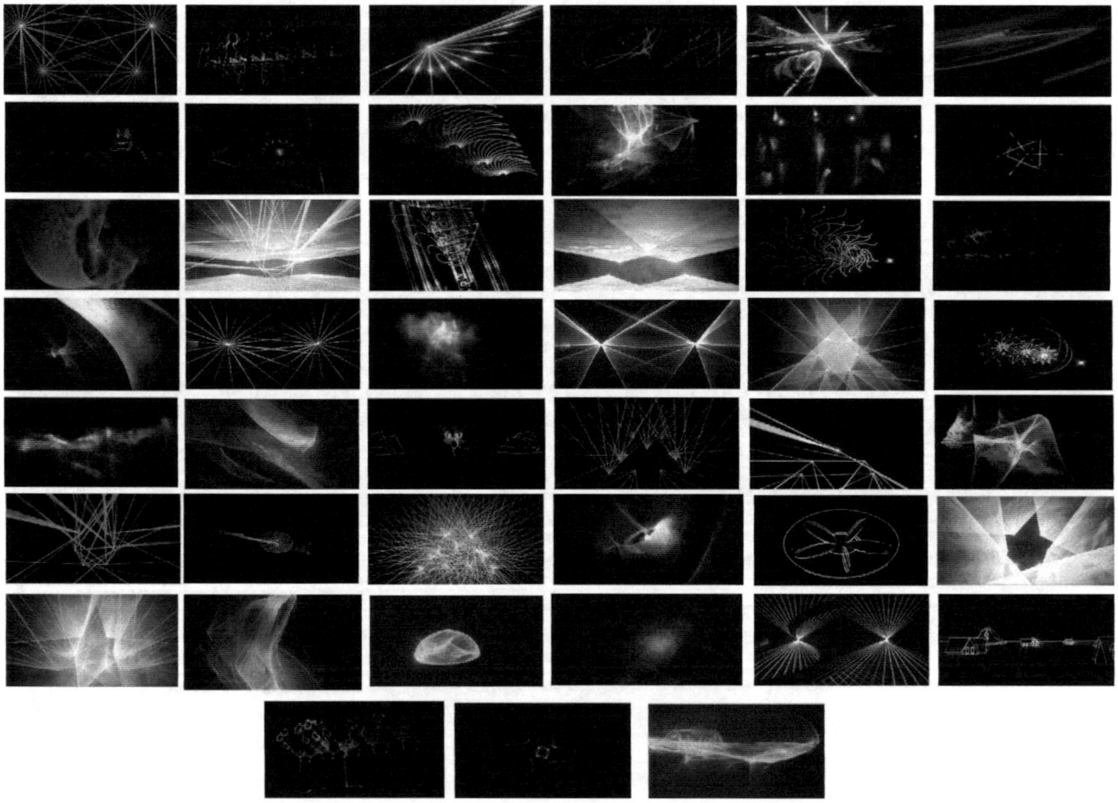

Fig. 1. Laser show images

One hundred and sixty-one participants (men and women aged 17-48 years) in took part in the study. Of these, 44 participants were from the art field and 117 participants did not have any artistic background. Laser show images were presented to the respondents in random order. The participants were asked to rate their emotional and relaxation experience and the attractiveness of the laser show images on a scale from -2 to +2. Next, we applied the fractal theory in order to establish a relationship between the visual complexity of laser show pictures and their human visual perception. The "box-counting" dimension D was calculated for our images using an image-processing software ImageJ (ImageJ, 2016). The color pictures were converted to black and white (monochrome) images using the Canny edge detection algorithm (Canny, 1986). The obtained images were placed on a grid scale, in which all boxes had a fixed size ε. The number of boxes $N(\varepsilon)$ that the image crossed was counted by using the ImageJ software. Next, we reduced the size of boxes and repeated the procedure several times. The fractal dimension D was determined from the slope of the graph, where the x-axis was the $\log(\varepsilon)$ and the y-axis was $\log(N(\varepsilon))$.

Thus:

$$D = -\,\mathrm{tg}\alpha \qquad (2)$$

where α is the angle of the slope.

We calculated *D* values of all pictures for different types of laser effects (Table 1).

Table 1. *D* values of laser show pictures for different types of laser effects

Type of laser effect	D_{min}	D_{max}	D_{mean}
Lumia effects	1.296	1.657	1.490
Beam effects	1.198	1.621	1.333
Screen effects	1.065	1.587	1.331

Next, we calculated the Spearman correlation coefficients (Wayne, 1989) between *D* values of the laser show pictures and the respondents' reaction to them (Table 2).

Table 2. The correlation between *D* values of the laser show pictures and the respondents' reaction to different types of laser effects

Type of laser effect	Spearman correlation coefficient		
	Attractiveness	Emotional effect	Relaxation effect
Lumia effects	-0.286	-0.120	-0.283
Beam effects	0.211	0.202	-0.019
Screen effects	0.110	0.119	0.039

3 Results and discussion

The results of our calculation showed that lumia show pictures had maximum values of fractal dimension (D_{mean} = 1.499), whereas beam and screen show pictures had approximately equal *D* values (D_{mean} = 1.333 and D_{mean} = 1.331, accordingly). Thus, lumia show pictures are more complex than beam and screen ones.

The low correlation between the visual complexity of pictures and the respondents' reaction to them exposes individual preferences for abstract images. The negative correlation coefficients obtained for the lumia effects and the positive relation established for the beam effects are of great importance and point to the following:

1. On the one hand, the structure of the lumia show pictures is complex (the maximum *D* value falls within the low preference range and the minimum *D* value is close to the high preference range) so the respondents preferred simpler lumia effects;

2. On the other hand, the minimum *D* value of the beam show pictures is below the high preference range, so the respondents preferred more complex beam effects.

The obtained results support the theory of a relationship between the fractal dimension and aesthetic judgment (Forsythe et al., 2011; Mureika, 2005; Taylor et al., 2007; Abbott, 2017; Taylor et al., 2001).

In our analysis, we did not take into account the color-grade of the pictures used. In addition, there were some problems with the binarization of the images, as the areas with solid color (generally, with intensity gradients) were interpreted as image "noise". On the one hand, the structure of images proved to more complex (the *D* value increased); on the other hand, the intensity gradients used for artistic expression affected the complexity of images. Further research is required to explore the impact of the intensity gradients on the visual complexity of the scene.

4 Conclusions

Our research has confirmed the relationship between the visual complexity of laser show pictures and their human psychophysiological perception. However, the individual preferences for abstract images are highly subjective. Therefore, the fractal dimension as such cannot define the aesthetic value of artworks. It should however be noted that the visual complexity of screen effects differs considerably from lumia to beam effects. Screen effects are more suited for the entertainment industry, whereas lumia and beam effects are more relevant for audiovisual art. The latter can be used to create the visual content for relaxation and anxiety management.

References

1. Abbott A. (2017). Fractal secrets of Rorschach's famed ink blots revealed. *Nature*. doi:10.1038/nature.2017.21473.
2. Bourke P. (2016). Fractals, Chaos. Retrieved 2016, from http://paulbourke.net/fractals/.
3. Canny J. A. (1986). Computational Approach to Edge Detection. *IEEE transactions on pattern analysis and machine intelligence*, *8* (5), 679-698.
4. Crownover R. M. (1995). Introduction to Fractals and Chaos. London: Jones and Bartlett Publishers, Inc., 306 p.
5. Daukantas P. (2010). A short history of laser light show. *Optics and Photonics News*, *21* (5), 42-47.
6. Forsythe A., Nadal M., Sheehy N., Cela-Conde C. J., Sawey M. (2011). Predicting beauty: Fractal dimension and visual complexity in art. *British Journal of Psychology*, *102* (1), 49-70.
7. ImageJ: Image Processing and Analysis in Java. Retrieved 2016, from https://imagej.nih.gov/ij/.
8. Lux Aeterna Theater. Retrieved 2017, from https://www.facebook.com/lux.aeterna.theater/.
9. Matveev N. V., Prokopenko V. T., Sapunova N. P., Fridman D. A. (2016). Research into the influence of light-music performances on psychophysiological states. *Light & Engineering*, *24* (2), 22-24.
10. Mental Rhythm. Devices for audiovisual stimulation. Russia. Retrieved 2016, from http://www.mentalritm.ru/pages/katsoftDVD2.html.
11. Mind Machines. USA. Retrieved 2016, from http://www.mindmachines.com/theta-minds-eye/.
12. Mureika J. R. (2005). Fractal dimensions in perceptual color space: A comparison study using Jackson Pollock's art. *Chaos*, *15* (2). 043702.
13. Taylor R. P., Guzman R., Martin T. P., Hall G. D. R., Micolich A. P., Jonas D., Marlow C. A. (2007). Authenticating Pollock Paintings Using Fractal Geometry. *Pattern Recognition Letters*, *28* (6), 695-702.
14. Taylor R. P., Newell B. R., Spehar B. Clifford C. (2001). Fractals: a resonance between art and nature? *Intersections of art and science. The Proceedings of Symmetry: Art and Science 1, Fifth Interdisciplinary Symmetry Congress and Exhibition of the International Society for the Interdisciplinary Study of Symmetry*, 194-197.
15. Theta Mind's Eye: Light and Sound Machine. Theta Voyager Light and Sound Machines. USA. Retrieved 2016, from http://www.thetavoyager.com/mind's%20eye.htm/.
16. Pangolin Laser Systems. Retrieved 2017, from http://pangolin.com/.
17. Wayne D. W. (1989). Applied nonparametric statistics. USA: Wadsworth Pub Co., 656 p.

Sky brightness measurements for different environmental conditions by the example of St. Petersburg

Svetlana Kolgushkina[1]

[1]ITMO University, School of Photonics, Faculty of Laser and Light Engineering, Department of Creative Lighting Design, St. Petersburg, Russia

Abstract. St. Petersburg is unique place in Russia with an environmental phenomenon called "white nights" during summertime: sky brightness levels are influenced mostly by environmental conditions. Sky conditions during the winter are opposite: light emission is mostly caused by the anthropogenic factors. A series of experiments were conducted between May and December 2017 using a Sky Quality Meter (SQM-LU-DL), a night sky brightness photometer, to understand the differences between sky brightness levels for different environmental conditions and seasonal variations. Sky brightness distinction between the city center and 20 km distance were estimated for clear sky conditions.

1 Introduction

Lighting design solutions in 21st century should be carried out with considering environmental conditions of place in order to improve its uniqueness. Sky brightness estimation during the night could show the distinctive features of different cities depending on locations. For example, near the equator duration of the night is about 12 hours both in winter and summer with insignificant duration of twilight. For the places near the North, at the same time, length of night strongly depends on the season. Transient moment between day and night is extended in time. Environmental influence on sky brightness is considerable during clear nights while artificial light impact more corresponds to cloudy weather conditions.

For field measurements documenting the evolution of sky brightness, different types of night sky brightness photometers, such as the Unihedron Sky Quality Meter, are widely used. [1,2] The SQM-LU-DL, a pocket-sized night sky brightness photometer with a data-logging system inside, was used to study St. Petersburg's artificial light emission. According to a published report of the relationship between the SQM photometrical system and the main systems used in light pollution studies, correction factors to CIE photopic and CIE scotopic were taken into account. [3,4]

[1] Corresponding author: svkolgushkina@corp.ifmo.ru

2 Field of study

The city of St. Petersburg is a very interesting example for corresponding research for a number of reasons: there are no laws, codes and standards in the Russian Federation for artificial light emission regulations and natural sky conditions change very significantly during the year: from high levels during summer time with a short period of dusk to a short daytime period during winter.

Changes in daylight hours during the year are very significant: on 22 December, the duration of the day in 2017 was 5h 53m while on 22 June it was 18h 50m. The dynamics of daylight changes from May to December are shown in Figure 1.

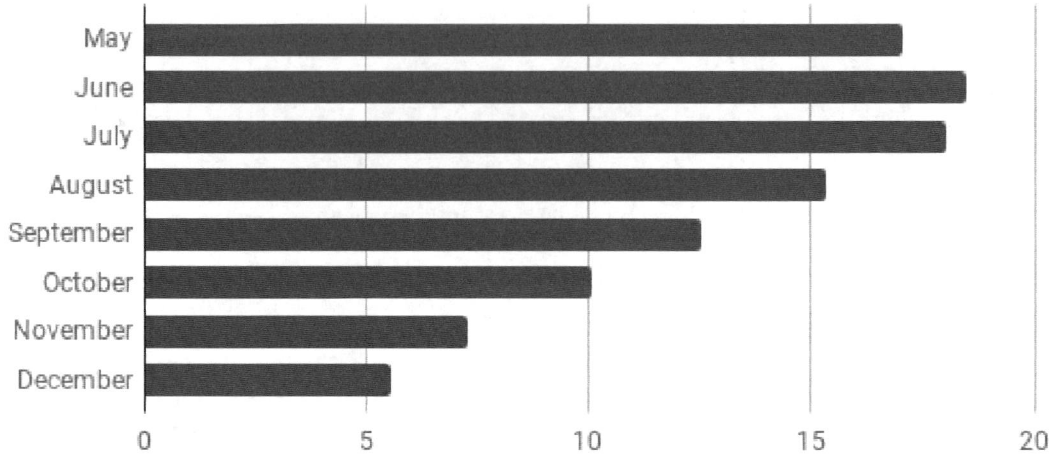

Figure 1. Dynamics of daylight hours during the period May - December 2017.

Night sky brightness is influenced by anthropogenic sky glow, which depends on weather conditions, background sky luminance, the position of the sun (indirectly scattered sunlight), and the phases of the moon. During the summer in St. Petersburg, luminance levels over the night sky are influenced mostly by environmental conditions, while during the winter, sky brightness levels are caused by artificial light emission on the molecules of water and aerosol. The quantity of overcast nights during December is 26 out of 31 days, while during June, it is 11 out of 31 days, as shown in Figure 2.

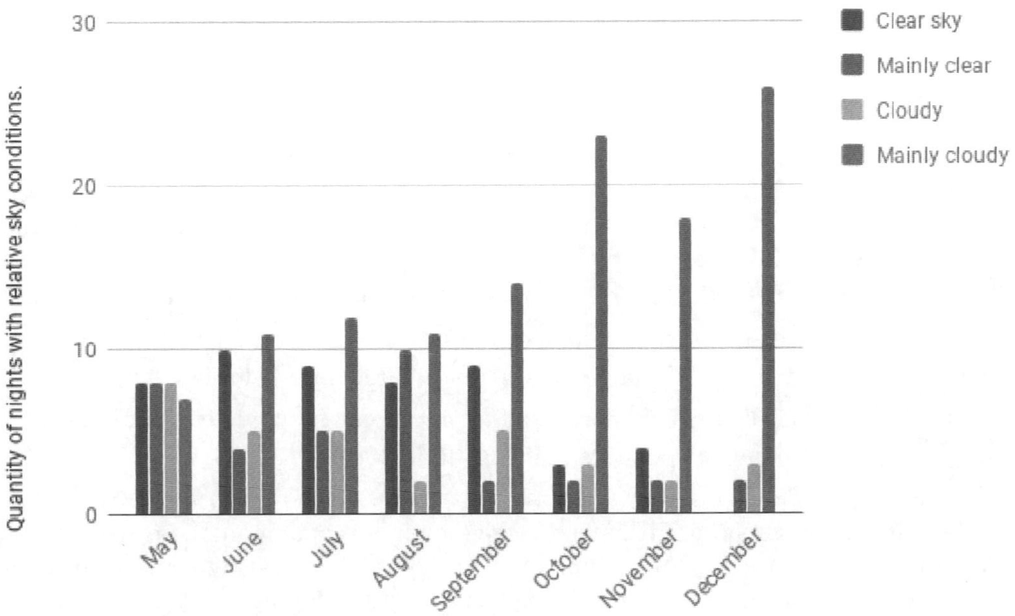

Figure 2. Quantity of nights with relative sky conditions.

The perception of sky conditions from the observer's perspective changes from summer to winter, as shown in Figure 3 and Figure 4.

Figure 3. Sky perception from the position of observer in June during "white nights".

Figure 4. Sky perception from the position of observer in December.

3 Methodology

For artificial light emission analysis there were used principles of modeling artificial sky brightness formed by Garstang in his model. 18 districts of St. Petersburg were considered separately.

In order to estimate sky brightness differences through the seasons series of field measurements were obtained using the Unihedron brightness photometer SQM-LU-DL aimed at quantitatively comparing and monitoring sky brightness through the night and night-to-night. The SQM-LU-DL device provides readings in magnitudes per square arcsecond $\frac{mag}{arcsec^2}$, a logarithmic measurement mostly used by astronomers to measure sky brightness. A decrease of magnitude value means an increase in the amount of light coming from a given patch of sky. A change of $5\frac{mag}{arcsec^2}$means a 100 time enlargement of the sky brightness. Each SQM-LU-DL is factory-calibrated. The absolute precision of each device is believed to be $\pm 0.10\frac{mag}{arcsec^2}$. The operating temperature range is -40 to $85C^0$.

A series of measurements were taken at the central side of the city between May - December 2017 at midnight for different weather conditions and moonphase at zenith angle zero in order to avoid influence of existing outdoor lighting fixtures. For each sky brightness analysis there were made series of measurements with data-logging every 5 seconds within 2 minutes which then were averaged. To compare sky brightness levels in the central part of the city with amount of light emission outside the city, a series of experiments were made 20 kilometres from the centre of the city. SQM-LU-DL was equipped with the lens at half width half maximum (HWHM) of the angular sensitivity (~10°). The block diagram of the device is shown Figure 5 and Figure 6.

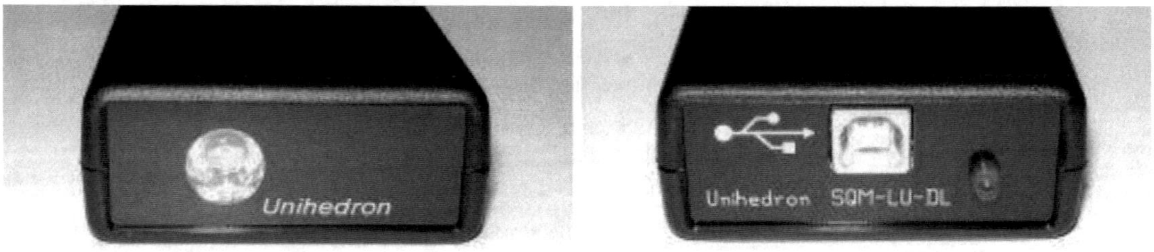

Figure 5. SQM-LU-DL device with a data-logging system inside.

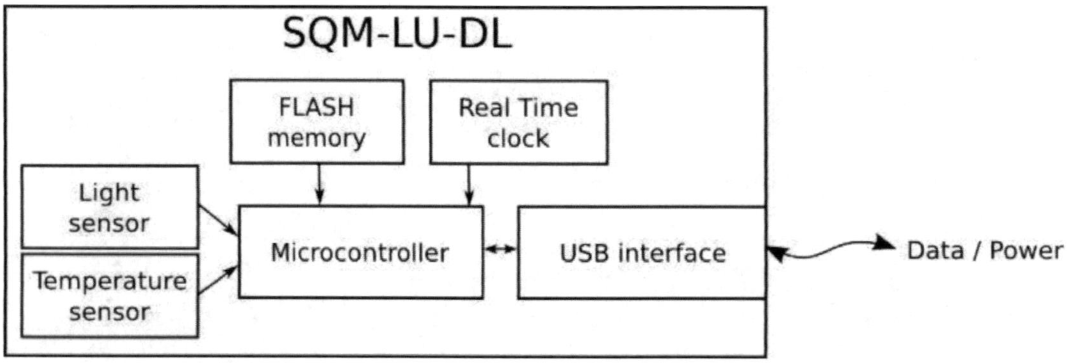

Figure 6. SQM-LU-DL device block diagram.

To convert the SQM Magnitudes per square arcsecond readings to $cd/m^2$the following equation (1) was used in accordance with manufacturer's data:

$$[cd/m^2] = 10{,}8 \times 10^4 \times 10^{(-0{,}4\times[mag/arcsec^2])} \quad (1)$$

According to the calculations made by P. Cinzano aimed at evaluating the relationship between the SQM photometric band and the CIE photometric system, the Sky Quality Meter is properly calibrated over Illuminant A. [3] P. Cinzano calculated spectral mismatch correction factors for the CIE photopic and scotopic responses as shown in Table 1. During the experiment, all of this information was taken into account.

Table 1. Spectral mismatch correction factors for CIE photopic and scotopic responses.

Light source	**HPS lamp**	**HPL lamp**	**Illuminant A**	**Sky natural**	**Sky polluted**	**Moon ab. atm**
Photopic	0,78	1,02	1,00	0,96	0,85	1,20
Scotopic	1,70	1,22	1,00	0,79	1,37	0,79

4 Results

During the on-field research there've been analysed night sky brightness depending both the lunar phase and artificial light emission for clear sky and cloudy weather conditions depending on the night. All the data in Magnitudes per square arcsecond were converted to the lighting metrics system. Data averaged for the midnights with different sky conditions and moon phases during the experiment are shown on the Figures 8-9.

The most influencing factor of artificial light emission is cloudiness. In December there were no clear sky nights and the level of brightness tends to have close values with the luminance on the roads. Moonlight influence is higher during clear nights than during cloudy nights. If there were no artificial light over the city, brightness of the overcast night would be lower, than the clear. But according to the measurements, sky during the overcast winter is brighter than during the shortest night of the year (June 22). Clear sky conditions with 0,5% Moon correspond to Minimum values during the month while overcasted sky with 95% Moon - to Maximum values. The dynamics of changes from May to December are shown in Figure 7 and Figure 8.

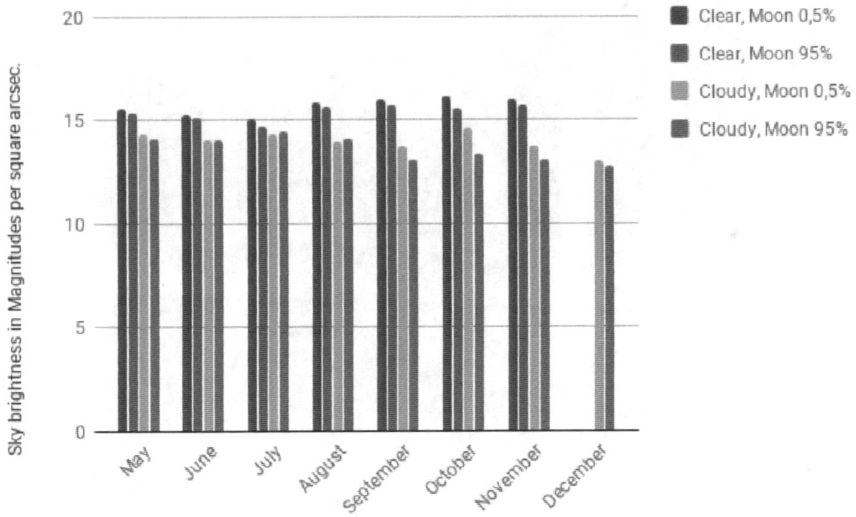

Figure 7. Sky brightness level depending on the month and sky conditions in Magnitudes per square arcsec at midnight between May - December 2017.

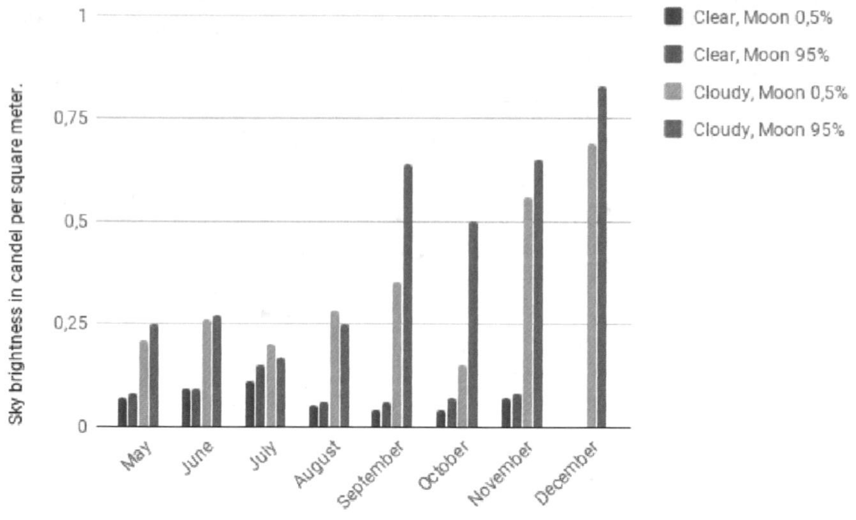

Figure 8. Sky brightness levels depending on the month and sky conditions in candela per square meter.

Comparing the measurements for clear sky conditions in the city center to the measurements for on 20 kilometers distance from the central side differences in values are shown in Figure 9.

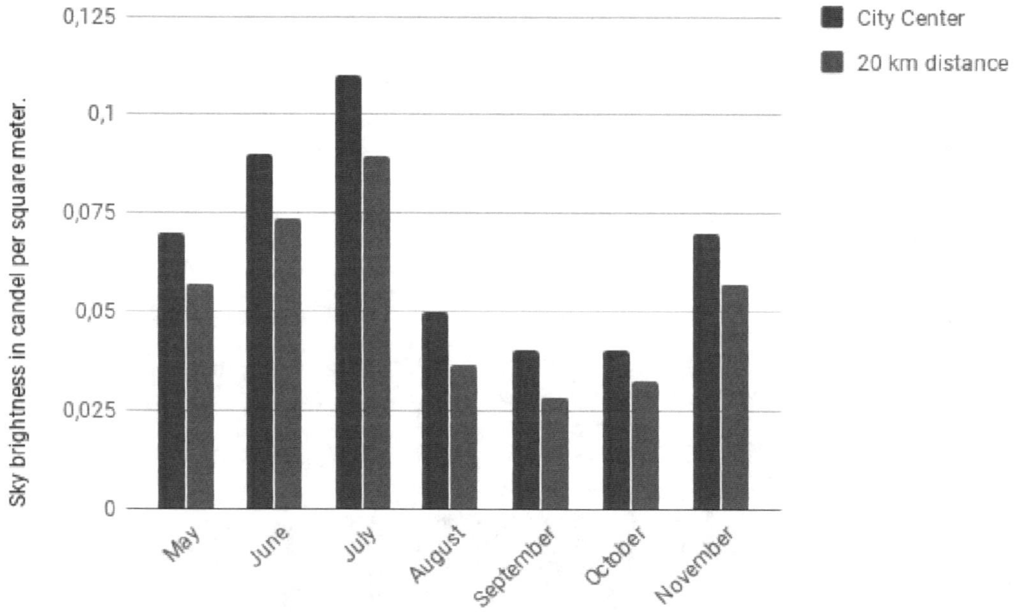

Figure 9. Sky brightness for clear sky conditions in the city center and on 20 km distance without moonlight.

The differences in sky brightness values between the city center and 20 km distance for clear sky conditions are about 17-21% depending on the month.

Statistical analysis of measurements for midnight sky brightness between May - December 2017 refers to the following results: during clear and moonless sky conditions night sky brightness at St. Petersburg reaches values during summer 15,03 - 15,55 $\frac{mag}{arcsec^2}$in transition to lighting metrics 0,07 - 0,11 cd/m^2.

During the winter values for clear sky are close to 15,45 - 16,1$\frac{mag}{arcsec^2}$in transition to lighting metrics 0,04 - 0,07 cd/m^2. Overcast sky is mainly caused by the scattering process on aerosols and moleculas and sky brightness levels are always higher than during the clear sky nights and reaches the values 14,28 - 12,82 $\frac{mag}{arcsec^2}$ (0,21 - 0,83 cd/m^2).

5 Conclusions

Sky brightness during the night is an important link among environmental aspects and perception from perspective of observer. Sky glow is approaching by value to luminance levels on the roads' surfaces with significant impact on adaptation and could be considered as a factor influencing on perception of contrast.

Brightness levels, as litmus paper for lighting design needs, could help to evaluate both natural conditions of night sky and contribution to sky glow of existing lighting in order to identify:

- environmental identity of place
- potential ways for further development of lighting design in the cityscape

All of these aspects have clear prospects in lighting design. For example, natural sky estimation could be used for development of integrated lighting control systems with respect to environmental changes. Corresponding solutions are potentially interesting for St. Petersburg and the other North cities with similar environmental phenomenons.

Considering the impact of existing lighting to sky glow, critical values could be evaluated. Then, if sky brightness is higher than critical, special codes and standards recusing sky glow should be developed. This approach is relevant for a large number of cities, especially metropolises, with a significant leap in quantity of lighting in recent years.

References

1. Birriel, J. Documenting Local Night Sky Brightness Using Sky Quality Meters: An Interdisciplinary College Capstone Project and a First Step Toward Reducing Light Pollution *Publication of JAAVSO Volume 38,* **2010**, 132-138
2. Benn, C. R., & Ellison, S. L. Brightness of the night sky over La Palma, *New Astronomy Reviews*, **1998**, 503–507.
3. Cinzano P. Night sky photometry with sky quality meter. *Internal Report n. 9, v.1.4*; Istituto di Scienza e Tecnologia dell Inquinamento Luminoso (ISTIL); **2005**.
4. Lolkema, D., Haaima, M., den Outer, P., & Spoelstra, H. 2010, Effects of atmospheric conditions on night sky brightness, *Tech. rep., National Institute for Public Health and the Environment, RIVM Report 680151002*, **2010**

Artificial light emission analysis for the city of St. Petersburg

Svetlana Kolgushkina[1]

[1]ITMO University, School of Photonics, Faculty of Laser and Light Engineering, Department of Creative Lighting Design, St. Petersburg, Russia

Abstract. Artificial light emission within the limits of major cities is increasing year by year. The level of this rapid growth depends on the influence of complex factors such as urban enlargement, air pollution, environmental conditions, lack of outdoor lighting master-planning, etc. Continuing monitoring of sky glow changes is an important part of the lighting environment's complex analysis. This paper estimates the contribution of 18 districts of St. Petersburg to the glow between 2014 and 2017, evaluated with the use of Garstang's model and GIS-based analysis of VIIRS data. The dynamic changes in sky brightness show a significant increase in the anthropogenic sky glow over three years.

1 Introduction

The influence of urban lighting on night sky brightness has been studied since 1970s. The first model for a sky brightness estimation was Walker's model [1]. Walker's law is described by the equation (1), considering the population size and the distance of the observer from the city.

$$B = CPD^{-2,5} \tag{1}$$

where P is the population, D is the distance of the observer from the city, B is an increase in the sky brightness related to natural sky glow, and C is the coefficient dependent on such factors as light emission per capita and the reflection coefficient of the ground surface.

A more complex model of sky brightness estimation, which took into account the approximation for small angles and considered the mechanisms of particle dispersion, was proposed by Bertiau and Treanor [2]. Treanor's model was modified by Garstang [3,4,5] to consider the heterogeneity of the atmosphere. In the modified model, the density of molecules and aerosols in the atmosphere exponentially decreases with altitude increase. Garstang's model showed itself as responsive in many American observatories. Since 2001, satellites have been used to analyse artificial night sky brightness. This research was first published by P. Cinzano, F. Falchi and C. D. Elvidge.

[1] Corresponding author: svkolgushkina@corp.ifmo.ru

The problem of artificial light emission growth has traditionally been tackled by astrophysicists and astronomers. Yet experts from other related fields have been lately paying increasing attention to this problem.

From the lighting design perspective, artificial light emission analyses are very important to monitor annual augmentation in order to protect the environment from the further growth of sky glow caused by artificial lighting in the cityscape. This is especially important for countries without control over the minimization of light pollution.

2 Field of study

Despite the importance of limiting artificial light emission, this question has not been sufficiently studied in Russia. A lack of specific requirements, which would limit and regulate the work of lighting designers, amplifies the problem.

Figure 1. An example of a low-quality lighting solution.

Figure 2. Luminance distribution, measured by using a luminance measuring imaging photometer.

Changes in the number of light fixtures between 2014 to 2017 is shown in Table 1.

Table 1. The number of light fixtures (Data source: State Unitary Enterprise Lensvet)

Year	Number of fixtures	Number of poles	Objects with arch. lighting
2014	215319	78508	427
2017	257600	97696	445

Table 2. The share of light fixtures in 2017 (Data source: State Unitary Enterprise Lensvet)

Types of light sources	% of the total	% of capacity
HPS lamps	65.4	87.6
Metal halide lamps	26.6	10.3
LED lamps	8.44	1.94

The number of lighting fixtures grew by 42,000 units between 2014 and 2017. In view of these significant changes, the analysis of dynamic artificial light emission is of utmost importance.

In the Russian Federation, there are no laws, codes or standards, which would regulate light pollution. The number of buildings and constructions with architectural lighting in big cities in Russia is very high, compared with European countries. To raise the issue of light quality, we evaluated sky glow progression in the period between 2014 and 2017.

3 Methodology

In our study, we used artificial sky brightness modelling principles formulated by Garstang. In total, 18 districts of St. Petersburg were considered separately and included in the research study.

Garstang's model offers a two-component composition of the atmosphere [4,5]:

- molecular components of the atmosphere, which particle density at h height above the sea level is described by the equation:

$$N_1(h) = N_m \cdot e^{-c(h)} \qquad (2)$$

where $N_m = 2.55 \cdot 10^{19}$ sm^3 *is the particle density at sea level,* $c = 0.104$ km^{-1} *according to Allen*

- aerosol particles, which density at h height is:

$$N_2(h) = N_a \cdot e^{-a \cdot h} \qquad (3)$$

where $N_a = 2.55 \cdot 10^{19}$ sm^3 *is the density of aerosol particles at ground level,* $a = 0.657 + 0.059K$ *is the approximation based on McClatchey data, K indicates the quality of the atmosphere. [4,5]*

The equations 3 and 4 may be used with the following assumptions:

- molecules in the atmosphere are in hydrostatic equilibrium
- density of aerosol is the exponential function

- the atmosphere is horizontally homogeneous

The absorption in the lower layers of the atmosphere for vertical distribution of particles is represented by the Lambert-Beer law.

$$\tau(h) = \int_0^h kdh = N_m \cdot \sigma_m \cdot [(1 - e^{-ch})c^{-1} + 11.778K(1 - e^{-a'h})] \tag{4}$$

where $k = N_m \cdot \sigma_m + N_a \cdot \sigma_a$, σ_m *is cross section of the molecules,* σ_a *is cross-section of aerosol particles.*

The model considers Rayleigh scattering of molecules in the atmosphere with the cross-section of $\sigma_R = 4.6 \times 10^{-27} sm^2$ for the 550 nm wavelength for visible observations. Multiple scattering of molecules and aerosol particles is described by the equation:

$$SAA(\omega) = N_m \sigma_m (11.778K \frac{\{1 - e^{-ascos\,\psi}\}}{a} + \gamma \frac{\{1 - e^{-cscos\,\psi}\}}{c}) cos\,\psi^{-1} \tag{5}$$

where γ *is the Garstang factor to account for the spherical nature of Rayleigh scattering compared to aerosol scattering [4,5].*

According to Garstang's model, artificial light emission intensity distribution in the upper hemisphere is described by the equation:

$$I_{up} = \frac{LP}{2\pi} \cdot \{2G(1 - F) \cdot cos\psi + 0.554 \cdot F \cdot \psi\} \tag{6}$$

where G is the surface albedo, F is the proportion of the luminous flux emitted by light fixtures into the upper hemisphere, P is the population, L is luminous flux per capita.

Luminous flux per capita was estimated based on statistical data on lighting equipment provided by State Unitary Enterprise Lensvet. The population size of 18 districts was evaluated in accordance with Federal State Statistics Service data.

In the equation (6), the albedo of the earth's surface was set G=0.15, and the proportion of the luminous flux emitted by lamps into the upper hemisphere is F=0.13.

The basic equation of the sky brightness model is:

$$b = \pi \cdot I_{up}(\psi) \cdot S^{-2} \cdot \int du \cdot e^{-\tau(s)} \cdot (1 + SAA) \cdot e^{-\tau(u)} \tag{7}$$

The formula for the transition to photometric units, accepted in astronomy, is as follows:

$$V = 41.438 - 1.0857 \cdot ln(b) \tag{8}$$

For GIS-based analysis, we used different layers of information about St. Petersburg, such as residential population data, Visible Infrared Imaging Radiometer Suite (VIIRS) data on radiance provided by the Earth Observation Group, and National Geophysical Data Center (NOAA) collected by Jurij Stare.

Figure 3. The residential population data layer.

4 Results

The largest contribution to the increase in the sky brightness in St. Petersburg is made by the following regions: Kalininsky, Primorsky, Vyborgsky, and Nevsky.

The artificial light emission data obtained for all districts are shown in Figure 4 and Table 3.

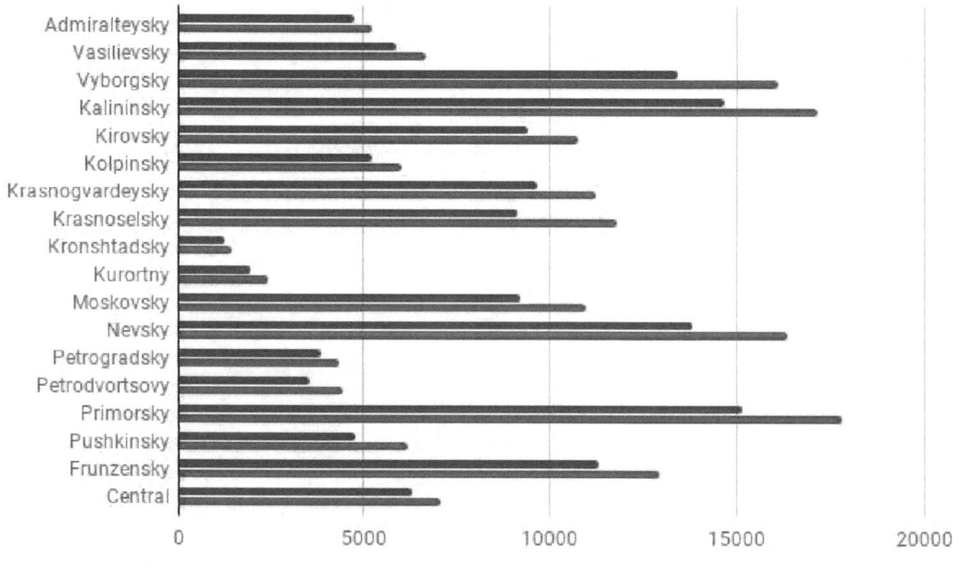

Figure 4. The artificial light emission data obtained for all districts of St. Petersburg based on Garstang's model for the years 2014 (blue bars) and 2017 (red bars).

Table 3. The population and artificial light emission intensity for 18 districts of St. Petersburg.

District	2014		2017	
	P, thousands of	I_{up} , cd	P, thousands of	I_{up} , cd

	people		people	
Admiralteysky	171	4762	164	5242
Vasilievsky	211	5875	209	6694
Vyborgsky	483	13449	502	16096
Kalininsky	527	14674	536	17134
Kirovsky	339	9439	337	10776
Kolpinsky	187	5207	188	6003
Krasnogvardeysky	348	9690	352	11250
Krasnoselsky	330	9189	370	11833
Kronshtadsky	44	1225	44	1423
Kurortny	70	1949	76	2434
Moskovsky	333	9272	344	11006
Nevsky	498	13869	512	16368
Petrogradsky	139	3870	136	4340
Petrodvortsovy	128	3564	138	4420
Primorsky	544	15147	556	17772
Pushkinsky	172	4789	193	6182
Frunzensky	408	11360	406	12993
Central	227	6320	220	7047

The results of the GIS-based analysis for the period between 2014 and 2017 are shown in Figure 5 and Figure 6.

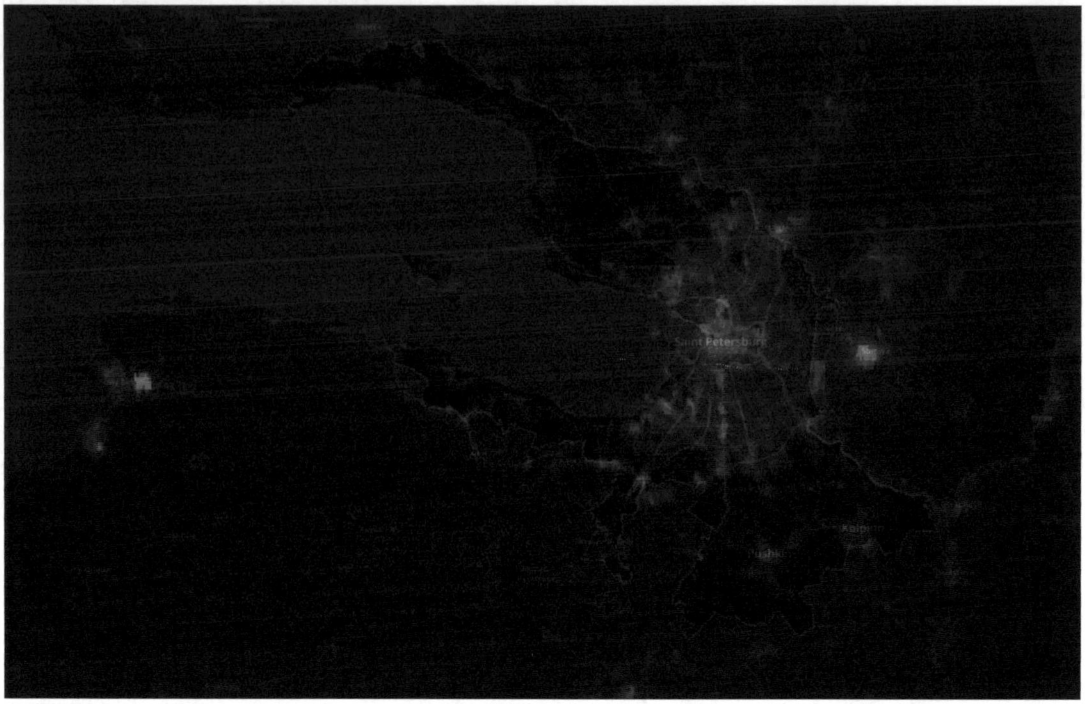

Figure 5. Artificial light emission data obtained for all districts of St. Petersburg based on 2014 statistical data.

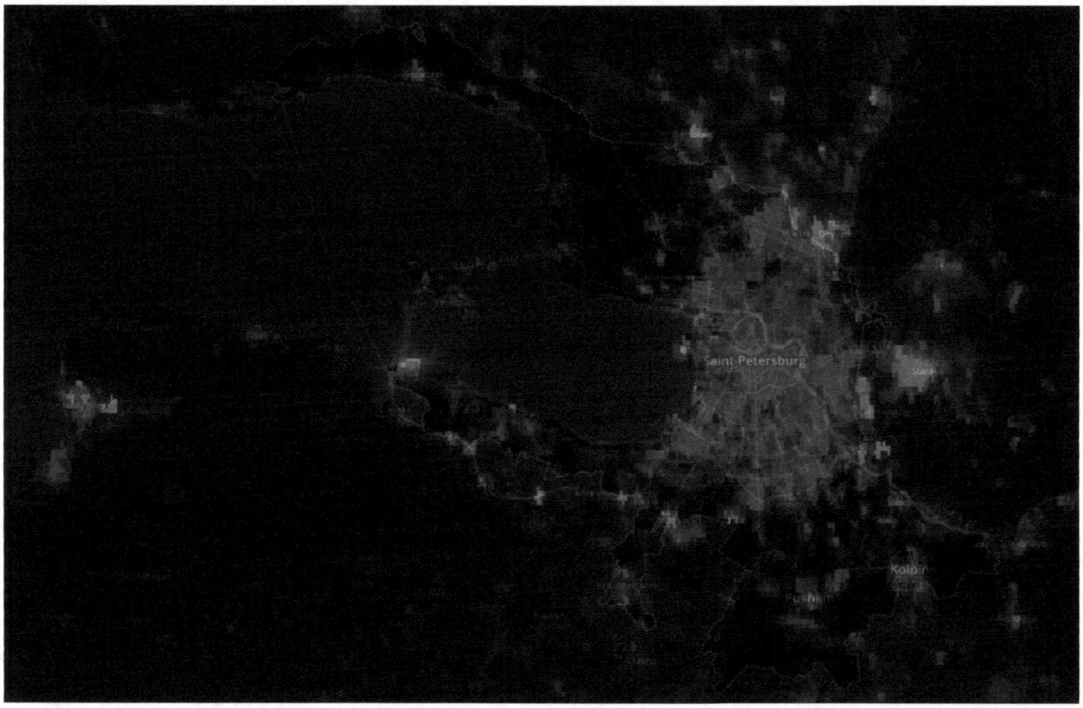

Figure 6. Artificial light emission data obtained for all districts of St. Petersburg based on 2017 statistical data.

5 Conclusion

Artificial light emission is growing very rapidly without any codes or laws which would help minimize light pollution. The attention of lighting designers should be focused on the quality of their work.

According to the definition of the Institution Lighting Professionals (ILP), any artificial light, which goes beyond the limits of the subject to illumination, including the light projected above the horizon into the night sky or creating glow danger, is considered undesirable and causes light pollution.

At present, some countries such as the Republic of Chile, Slovenia, Italy, the Czech Republic, parts of the United States of America and the United Kingdom have adopted a series of regulatory documents with the aim to reduce the anthropogenic component of sky glow.

To reduce the dynamics of the growth in anthropogenic component of sky glow, patterns of light propagation in the lower layers of the atmosphere and scattering type of various particles should be considered while design works. The reflected component of the light flux from the surfaces to be illuminated contributes significantly to sky glow. Therefore, light pollution can be reduced by optimizing the design of lighting systems, ensuring their compliance with acceptable levels of quantitative characteristics of lighting, performing installation control, and using lighting control systems.

References

1. Walker, M. F. The Effects of Urban Lighting on the Brightness of the Night Sky. *Publ. Astron. Soc. Pacific* **1977**, *89*, 405–409.
2. Bertiau, F. C., de Graeve, E. Treanor, P. J. The Artificial Night-Sky Illumination in Italy. *Vatican Observatory Publ.* **1973**, *1*, 159−179.
3. Garstang, R. H., *Light Pollution Modeling, 1991 in Light Pollution, Radio Interference, and Space Debris*, ISBN 0-937797-36-8; D.L. Crawford, Bookcrafters, Inc., 56−69.
4. Garstang, R. H. Model for Artificial Night-Sky Illumination. *Publication of the Astronomical Society of the Pacific* **1986**, *98*, 364–375.
5. Garstang, R. H. Night-Sky Brightness at Observatories and Sites. *Publ. Astron. Soc. Pacific* **1989**, *101* 306–329.

Living with Light: an ethnographic study of older people's use and experience of lighting at home

S.L.Nielsen[1] and M.F.Mullins [1]
[1] Aalborg University, Copenhagen, Denmark
stm@create.aau.dk mullins@create.aau.dk

Abstract. This ethnographic study aims to better understand the culture, values and everyday life of elderly people in view of their use of lighting in their homes. By addressing different types of lighting and exploring when, how and why older people used various lighting sources in their homes, the study seeks new insight into and an in-depth understanding of how older people experience light in their everyday lives. The paper introduces the results of a qualitative analysis of the collected data and presents some observations on the values and meanings the elderly attach to light and lighting in their daily lives. It is argued that these patterns are largely shaped by the elderly's bodily, social and cultural experiences and contexts, so a framework encompassing four major themes is proposed: 1. Traditions, Economy and Environment; 2. Quality of Life and Independence; 3. Health; and 4. Security and Safety.

1 Introduction

Aiming to develop better lighting-control tools for older people, the study seeks to better understand the culture, values and everyday life of older people living with lighting in their own homes. Through an examination of how many and what types of lighting sources older people have in their homes, when, how and why such sources are used, as well as how the elderly control and operate lighting, the project has sought new insight into and an in-depth understanding of how older people use and experience light in their everyday lives. The overall data and analysis of the report provide an indication of trends in lighting practices and the values of elderly people at home.

The study is part of a project, which seeks to address and remedy the challenges older people experience with the control of daylight and artificial light, particularly concerning programmable LED, circadian rhythm systems and other new technologies that are becoming widespread in Denmark. By asking the question of "How the elderly experience lighting in their everyday experience", the study employs ethnographic methods that, through a qualitative phenomenological approach, explore older people's experiences with lighting and their use of light in everyday life.

Two anthropologists facilitated three focus groups with 18 older citizens aged 61-80 years in cooperation with a local municipality. The citizens met at the Town Hall for an in-depth reflection and discussion of their everyday lives with light and lighting, focusing on their needs, wishes and ideas for the control and operation of light.

Prior to the focus group meeting, the participants had received three home assignments (or tasks), which they had been requested to prepare before the meeting. This form of data collection is inspired by design-anthropological methods (Gaver, Dunne, & Pacenti, 1999), which seek to open up participants' reflections on their everyday practices and experiences, in this case, with lighting at home.

The home assignments consisted of three tasks:

1. Where I live and where I have light
2. My day-today experience with light
3. Reflections about use of lighting in my home

The first assignment served as a form of mapping of the elderly's homes, where the elderly outlined a plan of their housing and its various forms, while specifying the place and number of light sources. The second task included a description of the space, activities and light sources the elderly used over 24 hours. Inspired by anthropological data collection methods on practice (Lange, 1988), the first and second home assignment thus worked together as a form of a guided tour for the participants' everyday life with light at home. The third task required the participants to complete a reflection sheet by answering the following questions:

1) In my everyday life, light means to me...?
2) Without light in my everyday life, I would...?
3) Light has a special significance for me when I...?

All 18 participants in the focus groups completed their three home assignments. The statistical and qualitative data obtained from the home assignments are based on 16 valid answers received from 17 older people and the data collected from the focus groups (18 participants).

Based on the home assignments, the focus groups were then used as an exploratory ethnographic method of translating, discussing and uncovering different values and practices that older people live with, and their connections to lighting at home. In particular, the study was interested in the meanings the target group attributed to lighting, their understanding of technical differences between LEDs and other light sources, as well as the link between light, aging and circadian rhythms (Sen et al., 2017).

Two anthropologists moderated the discussion in the group based on a questionnaire that allowed attitudes and views associated with home illumination to be debated; everyday experiences with light to be described and compared; and needs, wishes and ideas for the control of light to be discussed (Lange, 1988).

The first half of the focus group interview consisted of examining differences and similarities in the participants' answers to the home assignments. Here, the participants' values, habits, rhythms, routes and routines were associated with light in everyday life.

The second part of the focus group consisted in uncovering the current possibilities and limitations of the elderly for controlling the light in their homes, thereby exploring their needs, ideas, and wishes for controlling the light. A supplier[1] of lighting concepts and control systems for the healthcare sector had lent three different types of light controls that the elderly could study and discuss. Similar to the first part of the focus group, the participants' reflections and perspectives were facilitated by two anthropologists, with the help of a questionnaire.

The debates in the focus groups, together with the participants' answers to the home assignments, provide insights into the lives of the elderly with lighting at home. The processing and description of data has been structured through the distinction between light as a *materiality*, as a *practice* and finally as a *value*. Taken together, these distinctions form a picture of the lives of the elderly with light at home.

[1] Chromaviso A/S

2 Light as materiality in the home

2.2 Number and location of light sources in the home

The primary rooms of the elderly's homes include the entrance hall, living room, kitchen, bathroom, bedroom and work space. These rooms thus appear on all floor plans presented by the elderly as part of the first assignment.

The secondary rooms of the elderly's homes include the dining room, utility room / family room, guest room, hallway, staircase, terrace and / or orangery. Six of the elderly live in homes that include these rooms, which can point to the elderly's housing situation – the size and partly type of housing (an apartment or a house).

The data show that 17 older people have 543 light sources in their homes - an average of 32 light sources per home. Generally, data shows that the biggest number of light sources used by the older people are located in the living room. In total, 17 older people have 115 light sources in their living rooms, an average of seven light sources per living room, ranging from max. 14 to minimum two sources. This observation largely depends on the fact that the living room is typically the largest and most multifunctional home space. In other words, the living room serves for more elderly people as a room that provides a framework for several types of practices that consequently require different types of lighting.

The kitchen is a place, where the second biggest amount of light sources is concentrated, with 84 light sources combined. The average of five light sources per kitchen, according to the data collected from the focus group interviews, is often due to the location of skylights and spots in the ceiling and under the kitchen cabinets, respectively. In the bedroom, the elderly have, on average, three light sources located, primarily in the form of one skylight and several reading lamps.

Halls and bathrooms are the rooms generally contain relatively few light sources. In addition, there is a tendency for secondary rooms in the homes of the elderly (e.g. corridors, stairs, guest rooms, dining rooms and utility rooms) to accommodate between 11 to 25 light sources in total.

2.3 The nature of home light sources

As part of the first home assignment 1, the elderly were asked to indicate the nature of their light sources in their homes, subjectively classifying them as 'sharp', 'less sharp' or 'weak'. Overall, the home assignments showed that the elderly primarily see their homes as mostly using sharp light sources (227 light sources), followed by less sharp light sources (196 light sources) and less sharp light sources (111 light sources).

According to the elderly's feedback from the focus group, when it comes to the nature of the home light sources, a distinction is made between "functional lights" and "cozy lights", or "mood lights". The elderly thus expressed their preferences in terms of how they placed and used different types of light sources to support them in different activities and moods at home.

The distribution of different types of home light sources by the elderly shows a tendency for the placement of predominantly sharp light sources in the rooms with a specific fixed functionality, such as cooking in the kitchen and working in the office space. The living room and bedroom, on the other hand, are characterized by a preponderance of medium-glare sources and an almost even distribution between sharp and soft lighting, which defines this space as more fluid, where more varied activities can take place.

In relation to the nature of light sources at home, a tendency for a specific light culture among the elderly was detected, with the majority of the elderly having light placed on / in shelves and onto paintings, although, according to several participants, this is a sign of "belonging to the generation that came before us". In addition, participants mentioned the challenge in finding compatible light sources for the PH[2] lamps that many have in their homes. This "PH problem", as one could call the challenge, arises, as one elderly participant explained, in the encounter between the diffusion of light in the lamp design, the brightness of the light source and the heat released by the luminaire. The new types of light sources, such as LEDs, are simply unable to deliver a sufficiently high quality of light through the PH lamp luminaire and often overheat. In addition, the participants also explained how the quality of light in many of the new light sources did not have sufficient color reproduction allowing one to distinguish between various colors and patterns when, for example, knitting or sewing. The PH problem was generally addressed by the older men during the focus groups, and the female participants expressed their opinion that the PH lamp light is of poor quality.

The attitudes to sharp and cold light vs. soft and warm light were also reflected in the participants' answers to the third assignment. For example, one participants provided the following response to the question: 'Light had a special significance for me when I ...?'"Modern cars with sharp LED white / bluish light dazzle me on the dark road. A Christmas tree with warm electric lighting makes me happy. If it has a bright white / bluish light, it does something negative to me ..." Another participant mentioned how her neighbour had once pointed out how much glare the light in the kitchen gave. Since then she was therefore extra careful to use this light. Another participant, in contrast, said that he appreciated the "warm blue light", which may be due to the fact that he earlier lived in Asia, so he had a higher degree of exposure to this type of lighting.

Thus, the specific patterns and values of different forms of light among the elderly were observed, which can be understood, inter alia, in the context of gender, social and cultural background.

3 Light as a practice in the home

The qualitative data regarding the number and types of light sources the elderly have at home, hides a more qualitative, phenomenological insight into the ways the elderly use light sources in practice and how they inhabit their homes.

In order to address and understand the role and importance of the home lighting for the elderly, and based on this input create lighting controls suitable for the elderly, it is essential to address the home as a cultural phenomenon and a context for their everyday life with light.

From an anthropological, phenomenological perspective, home is not something you have, but something you do. In other words, a home "happens" through human beings dwelling in physical frameworks, as a relational process between humans and materiality, where people through their own rhythms, routes and routines allocate physical frameworks and life in themselves (Ingold, 1995).

In this understanding of the concept of home, lighting and the control of light in the home of the elderly thereby not only expresses a limited materiality but more importantly, comprise elements within a larger whole with which the elderly can inhabit their physical surroundings. Ultimately, lighting assists people to shape their experience and meaning of home.

With this view in mind, data from the homework of the elderly and the statements in the focus group were analyzed through a study of both individual and ongoing rhythms, routes and routines, which in practice make up the lives of the elderly with light at home.

[2] Poul Henningsen lamp: PH lamps were originally designed in the 1920s, but are still very common among all age groups in Danish homes today.

3.1 Rhythms

When reviewing the participants' homework, we observed a tendency for a lack of active awareness about which, when and how many light sources are used. For example, where the elderly listed the light souces they used in the second homework assignment, generally these observations were made when the sources were turned on, rather than observing for how long they remained lit.

From another perspective, the feedback from the second homework assignment demonstrates that in practice the elderly use the light sources in the home as a form of background for living their lives, where lighting has merged with the background of their immediate awareness. In other words, the interaction with light seems to be based on what could be called a "course of behavior", where the use of light has become a matter of course and invisible to the elderly through repetitive rhythms and habits - just as people's use of materiality in everyday life generally seems to be (Latour, 1992; Miller, 2010).

3.2 Routes

To further understand the use of home light sources by the elderly, we carried out a mapping of the rooms that the participants used at various times of the day. This mapping indicated that the bedroom, bathroom, kitchen and living room are primarily used in the morning, whereas the living room, kitchen and office are used in the afternoon. The participants mainly (and almost only) use the kitchen and the living room in relation to cooking and dining, and from 7pm until bedtime the primary (and most importantly) used room is the living room. The rooms used late in the day are the living room, bathroom and bedroom, the latter from 10pm and later.

3.3 Routines

In addition to the continuous rhythms and routes that have appeared in the data relating to the elderly living with light, some participants in the focus group reported on their individual "home routines" in relation to their use of light. In the words of a participant: "When I get home, I always do my route and light candles ... I have my very particular rhythm". This special routine consisted of turning on the table lamps and lamps around the living room, as well as turning on the light in the workroom. Overall, the data obtained from both home tasks and statements from the focus group showed that the elderly illuminate the rooms that they use actively both as a way to illuminate the space used and as a way to create an overview of their surroundings. One participant explained it -as follows:"It's a bit like when I turn on the lights in the corners of the living room .. you just need to create a place. it gives a sense of security". In addition, some participants mentioned how the "lighting the lights" always happens when guests are visiting.

These rhythms and routines are significant in forming the concept of 'being at home' and are important to include in the design of home lighting and lighting control.

4 Light as a home value

In the analysis of the assignments and debate in the focus group, several key themes and values emerged. These are the themes which seem to link the elderly's experience, understanding and use of light at home.

4.1 Tradition, environment and economy

The majority of the participating elderly were surprisingly well informed and well versed about the recent developments of light sources and LED technology. In this context, it should be pointed out that the participating elderly as a group should not be considered uncritically representative of the older Danish population as a whole, as all of the participants had joined the focus groups on the basis of their interest in lighting control at home.

Despite their knowledge of and use of new LED technology at home, the majority of the participants explained how they had experienced challenges with the recent years' technological transition from incandescent bulbs to LED bulbs. The elderly were generally fond of the traditional incandescent bulb that they had been used to and which "give such a nice warm light. The shift to a newer lighting technology was thus not compatible with values such as 'recognisability', 'usability' and 'tradition'.

In addition, many of the participants said that the new light sources could be difficult to integrate in their current lighting at home. This left several of the participants with a variety of lighting solutions at home, which some perceived as an irritating element.

Otherwise, the participants understood that the transition to LED bulb had led to greater economic savings, better environmental practices and a reduction in energy consumption. In addition, the participants reported that their participation in the focus group was based on their interest in gaining more knowledge about lighting and more strategies to live a " greener" life and lessen their impact on the environment with their individual light practices.

Thus, values such as 'recognizableness', 'usability', 'tradition', 'economical saving' and 'environment' are significant among the elderly in terms of their experience and use of light sources. In addition, the experience of poor light quality and high purchase prices seem to be among the perceived disadvantages of LED.

4.2 Life quality and personal control

The elderly explained how light is a central part of their everyday life, and how it supports their ways of home living. The elderly live with an experience and use of light as an essential element of staging and support of activities and moods at home.

Several older people pointed out how they used different light sources for different activities and moods. Bright light is most often used for the activities that focus on detail, such as cooking, reading and handiwork, whereas soft, reddish, "cozy lighting" is used in the living room in the evening and / or when there are visitors. One participant stated how "all activities go faster where the light complements them" and another expressed how she "... has bright light to work, read, knit and put make-up on; and more muted light to give coziness and security." More generally, others expressed how they would "feel the room uncomfortable and hard to read" and that it "would not work - neither for activities or for pleasure".

About half of the elderly had installed dimmers at home, especially in the living room, which for most people forms a framework for several different activities and serves as a scene for different moods. The distinction between the use of functional, mood lighting, and dimming possibilities in everyday life indicates that the elderly put a value in adjusting the lighting to suit them, the activity or the mood they are in or want to create. Thus, they broadly associate light with an experience of quality of life and wellbeing. Their experience of quality of life also seems to be connected to the opportunity and experience of personal control, and ability to adjust lighting. Flexibility and access to control of light is crucial to the elderly's experience of the quality of life associated with being the master of one's own house and one's own life.

4.3 Safety and security

The participants describe collectively how the light allows them to experience a sense of security in their own homes, both in terms of the confidence they experience with lighting at home in repeated bodily rhythms, routes and routines, but also through their ability to sense their surroundings and have a home.

In other words, the home's well-known practices and physical materiality provide an experience of safety for the elderly.

Additionally, light contributes to safety issues among the elderly in terms of accidents and falls. Proposals from both the focus groups and the home assignments showed how more elderly people had installed bright light at home. "I need to see the steps, so I do not stand on my heads going down the stairs", one participant said. Another participant mentioned how the fact that visual impairment made it difficult for her to navigate at home, with dim lighting.

4.4 Health and well-being

The data collected from the focus groups and the home assignments show how home lighting was influenced by the health of the elderly. Several of the elderly expressed that "light and well-being are connected". In particular, the influence of light on daily rhythm was something that emerged, largely linked to the daily rhythm of the natural light (Sen et al., 2017).

From the viewpoint of light as a practice, the opportunity for the elderly to control and adjust lighting through physical practice (see rhythms, routes and routines above) is not only significant in relation to the creation, maintenance and experience of home but is also significant in relation to the creation, maintenance and experience of health and well-being.

4.5 Summary

In general, the analysis of the collected data shows how older people use home light sources as a form of supportive background for their lives. To this end, the elderly themselves distinguish between basic, work and mood lighting, which they apply and adjust to their desires for activities and atmospheres, but which they often use simultaneously.

The recorded experiences provide an insight into what values and meanings the elderly attach to light in their daily lives, largely shaped by their bodily, social and cultural experiences and context. These values were grouped in the four categories: Traditions, Economy and Environment; Quality of Life and Independence; Health; and Security and Safety.

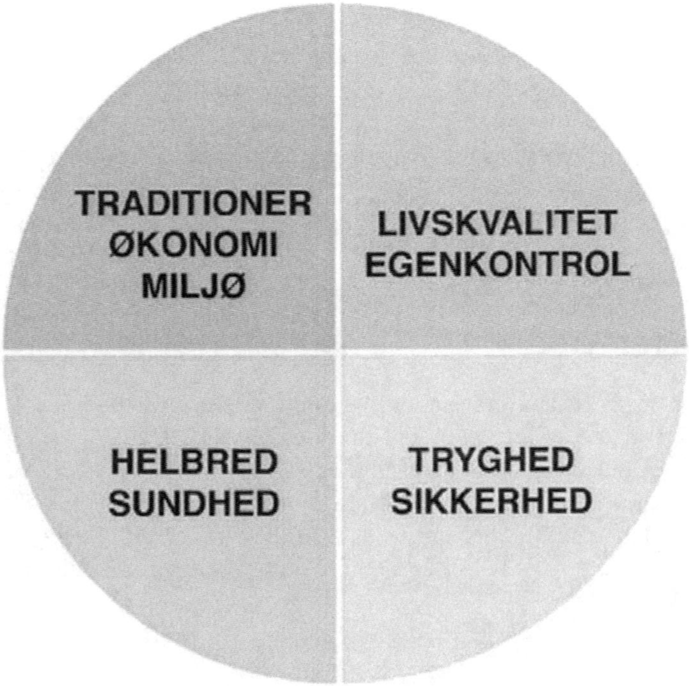

Figure 1: Model of Lighting Values for the Elderly

Experiences of technology, economy and environment were prominent and while several participants saw many benefits to technological development of lighting, the overall attitude was that the change seems to be too fast and does not offer any real useful advantage. In addition, participants experienced new lighting solutions as economically costly compared to what they have been used to; and they looked for information that would enable them to exploit the technologies toward greater care for the environment.

In addition, cognitive and sensory changes that accompany ageing play an important role, which designers need to take into account, in terms of safety and health.

5 Discussion

The qualitative data regarding the number and types of light sources the elderly have at home unveils a phenomenological insight into the way how elderly people use light sources in practice, and how light influences the way they inhabit their living space. In order to address and understand the role and importance of lighting for the elderly, and from there, create lighting controls, it is essential to address the home as a cultural phenomenon and context for their living of everyday life with light. From an anthropological, phenomenological perspective, home is not something one has, but something one does. In other words, a home "happens" through people's acquisition of, and dwelling in, physical frameworks - as a relational process between humans and materiality, where people allocate meaning to physical frameworks and life itself through their own rhythms, routes and routines.

The study's observations provide the insights, which are useful for the design and operation of lighting control for the elderly. An understanding of light as materiality, practice and value in the home of the elderly promotes awareness of the fact that lighting control is not a fragmented, isolated element in the everyday life of the elderly, but part of coherent everyday life and practice of home. The development of tools for controlling light thus can ultimately affect this greater context.

When creating light control technologies, the everyday home lighting practices can be changed, including the rhythms, routes and routines. Thus, lighting control has the potential to influence the practice of home, the experience of being-in-control, safety and security, as well as the sense of health and the overall quality of life among the elderly.

The development of light-controls for the elderly requires a particular ethical awareness and responsibility to protect and keep the user's home practice in mind. Lighting control devices should not be developed merely because technology allows it, but with a sense of sensitivity to and a desire for optimization and support for the reality that it shapes.

6 Acknowledgements

The authors wish to express their gratitude to the older citizens in Gladsaxe Municipality, who took the time to get involved in the assignments and the focus group. We are also grateful to Chromaviso for lending the equipment and to Gladsaxe Municipality's engagement and enthusiasm in organizing the focus group and providing the venue. In addition, we are thankful to anthropologist Nanna Hauge Kristensen for her constructive assistance during the study's data collection and processing. The study described in this paper is part of the project called 'Better Light - Better Operation', financed by the Danish Lighting Innovation Network.

References

Gaver, B., Dunne, T., & Pacenti, E. (1999). Design: Cultural probes. *Interactions*, 6(1), 21–29. https://doi.org/10.1145/291224.291235

Ingold, T. (1995). Building, dwelling, living: how animals and people make themselves at home in the world. In *Shifting contexts: Transformations in anthropological knowledge* (pp. 57–80).

Lange, B. K. (1988). Ethnographic Interview. *Occupational Therapy in Mental Health*, 8(2), 61–80. https://doi.org/10.1300/J004v08n02_05

Latour, B. (1992). Where are the missing masses, sociology of a few mundane artefacts application. In *Shaping Technology-Building Society. Studies in Sociotechnical Change* (pp. 225–259). Cambridge Mass.: MIT Press.

Miller, D. (2010). Theories of Things. In *Stuff* (pp. 42–78). Cambridge: Polity Press.

Sen, S., Flyvholm, A., Xylakis, E., Nielsen, S. M. L., Hansen, E. K., Mullins, M. F., & Triantafyllidis, G. (2017). Towards assessing the impact of circadian lighting on the well-being of the elderly from a holistic perspective. In *3rd International Conference on Architecture, Research, Care, Health* (pp. 1–20). Polyteknisk Forlag.

Educational complex of light-colored modeling of urban environment

Vladimir E. Karpenko[1,*]

[1]Far Eastern Federal University (FEFU), School of Engineering, Department of Architectural Environment and Interior Design, 8 Sukhanova St. Vladivostok 690090, Russia

Abstract. Mechanisms, methodological tools and structure of a training complex of light-colored modeling of the urban environment are developed in this paper. The following results of the practical work of students are presented: light composition and installation, media facades, lighting of building facades, city streets and embankment. As a result of modeling, the structure of the light form is determined. Light-transmitting materials and causing characteristic optical illusions, light-visual and light-dynamic effects (video-dynamics and photostatics), basic compositional techniques of light form are revealed. The main elements of the light installation are studied, including a light projection, an electronic device, interactivity and relationality of the installation, and the mechanical device which becomes a part of the installation composition. The meaning of modern media facade technology is the transformation of external building structures and their facades into a changing information cover, into a media content translator using LED technology. Light tectonics and the light rhythm of the plastics of the architectural object are built up through point and local illumination, modeling of the urban ensemble assumes the structural interaction of several light building models with special light-composition techniques. When modeling the social and pedestrian environment, the lighting parameters depend on the scale of the chosen space and are adapted taking into account the visual perception of the pedestrian, and the atmospheric effects of comfort and safety of the environment are achieved with the help of special light compositional techniques. With the aim of realizing the tasks of light modeling, a methodology has been created, including the mechanisms of models, variability and complementarity. The perspectives of light modeling in the context of structural elements of the city, neuropsychology, wireless and bioluminescence technologies are proposed. Conclusions are given on the environment-forming and transforming significance of artificial light and light technologies in the space of modern city. Light-colored modeling identity is expressed in methodical and figurative-artistic continuity in the use of techniques of light composition and optical art. The use of light composition contributes to the expression of local identity by means and techniques of light composition in the context of the image, "genius loci" using the example of the Vladivostok seaside city. Identity in psychology is expressed in the personal selection of the techniques of light composition, which are used in light-colored modeling.

1 Features of the educational complex of light-colored modeling of the urban environment

1.1 Structure of the educational complex

Methodological logic and the application of light effects in environmental design are accompanied by profound study of the laws of the psychology of visual perception, the theory of optical art [1] and light urbanism [2]. The structure of the educational complex includes a lecture block: modern visual art [3], psychophysiology, the theory of modern lighting design, lighting technology, a unit of practical works and virtual modeling. The structure of practical tasks includes several directions: creating a light composition, installation, media facade, lighting the facade of a building or street, creating a public pedestrian light environment.

1.1.1 Modeling of light form

The light form in art and lighting design can be defined as a form consisting of a series of transparent and opaque elements whose structure and main idea are revealed when using an artificial light source or light flux. Polychrome and monochrome radiation can participate in the formation of light volume and space with flooding or local lighting with a certain rhythm of light sources, light lines and a spot of light pattern. The following light-dynamic phenomena of the light

* Corresponding author: vekarpenko@gmail.com

form are singled out: 1.) the photostatic – a state of form fixed at the moment of invariability, revealing its light-shadow regularities, the values of brightness and contrast frozen in a drawing, outline and silhouette. Video-dynamics – the state of form changing, with a video sequence which allows researchers to study its movement, to program illumination changes, and to capture changes in the direction of the rays. The main purpose of this practical work is to study the features and the use of artistic means and techniques of op-art in creating a light composition. [1, 4]

The task of expressing optical illusion in a new modeled form is to create a three-dimensional or frontal light form, taking into account the shape formative (hue, colorfulness, lightness) and psychological (perception and interpretation) properties of the light and color by using mirror, glossy or matte surfaces. Various types of reflection are used as a means of visual transformation, expression of depth and planning, dynamics of reflections. These include: the superposition and overlapping of falling color and monochrome shadows that create a complex composite structure. The translucence effect and a narrow beam of light, created with the help of special materials, that form a characteristic light contour and pattern. The dynamics of changes in intensity, color and rhythm of luminescence over time, and the use of color filter reception that significantly change the aspect of the form.

Figure 1 shows some examples of light compositions (light forms) in educational and practical works. In the upper left image is a composition called "Composition 1" (A. Afonin). The work is made with cardboard and light-scattering elements (transparent plastic, rubber band of green color). The dimensions are: 220 x 300 x 50 mm, and it contains a light source LED strip (1 m). Its main idea is expressed in the distribution and dispersion of light through light-scattering elements. In the upper right image – the composition "Northern Lights" (P. Molinyova), is made with cardboard, foil and paper. The main idea is the optical effect of the Northern Lights created through the transfusion of light. The light coming from the flashlight is refracted, and projected onto the wall. The lower left image is the composition "Light Pyramid" (E. Bondarenko). The shape is made with paper, cardboard and LED light source (10 x 10 cm). The main idea is to create optical illusions and the effect of light scattering by filling the volume with a concentrated beam of light from a flickering LED. The lower right composition is called "Clouds" (S. Dorofeeva). It is made with foam board, matte plastic, two flashing LEDs, foil, and packing tape. The dimensions are 17,5 x 21,5 x 8 cm. The basic idea is to create a background flow of light from the source through the openings. Such a composition can be placed in window openings to create additional lighting effects in a room in daylight.

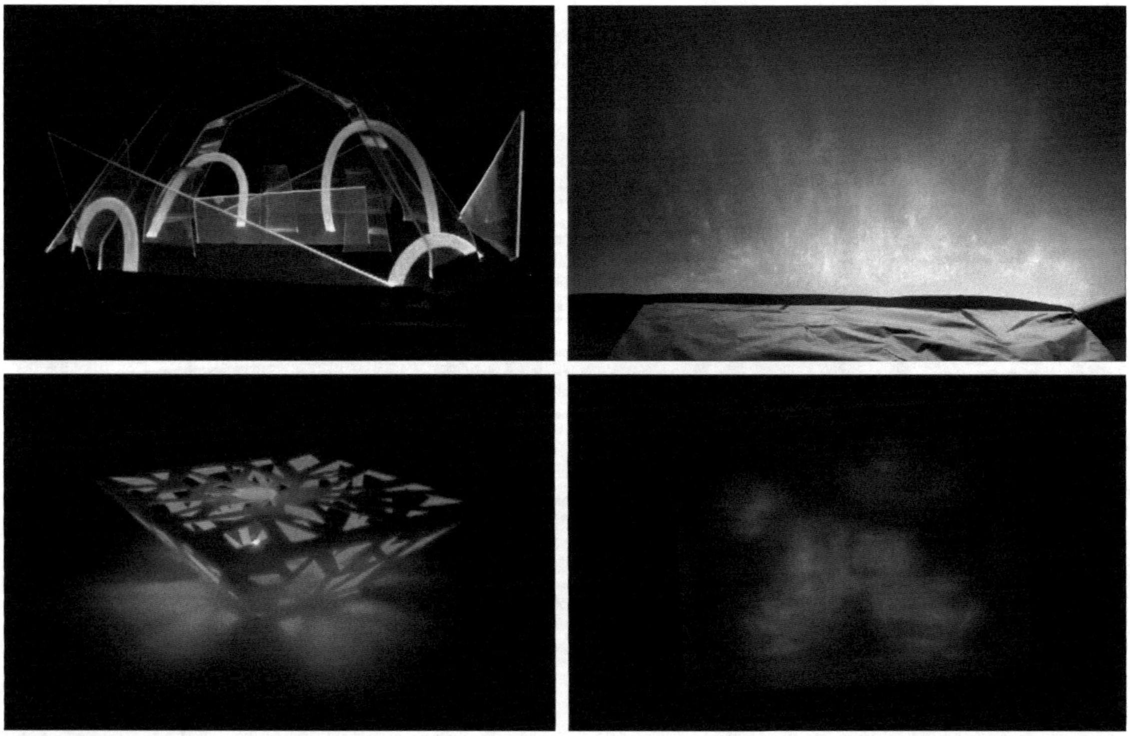

Fig. 1. Examples of light composition in practical educational works.

1.1.2 Modeling of light installation

Light installation is a form of modern visual art. It features a certain semantic content or artistic idea, expressed in voluminous and spatial composition created through artificial light, projection, animation, video and mechanical devices. Such an art form, usually large in scale, also includes an element of interactivity and active interaction with the observer. Technically it is achieved by using an electronic system: "sensor (touch, sound or motor) – processor – a person." Sensory recorders and computer processors are built into the installation design and form a single form. Modern techniques and means of light installation are expanded and become dependent, in many aspects, on scientific and technological achievements and social conditions. The main objectives of this practical work are to study the features, artistic means and techniques for creating a light installation using natural, artificial and other necessary light sources.

When modeling the educational light installation, prototypes were studied, artistic methods of their creation and the features of using light technologies in its composition were revealed, and the technical arrangement of the light installation space was considered. At the same time, various optical, psychological effects and illusions are revealed in the light form of the installations, taking into account the following: colorimetry parameters (hue, colorfulness, lightness), photometry (wavelength, P, (%), luminance – L (kcd/m^2)), reflection coefficients, refraction and absorption of materials, light dynamics and light animation [4]. The light installation "Comet" in Fig. 2 (left) shows techniques used to reflect the light form on water surface. The reflection effect complements the flickering circular image of the spiral, and is associated with the twisting motion of the cosmic body. The comet slides and leaves a cool blue light (E. Bondarenko, M. Borodavkina, S. Kucenko). In Fig. 2 (right), the light design of a fountain called "Lights of the Polar Star", the effect of the movement of water is recreated by directing the light rays from the fountain (A. Akimova).

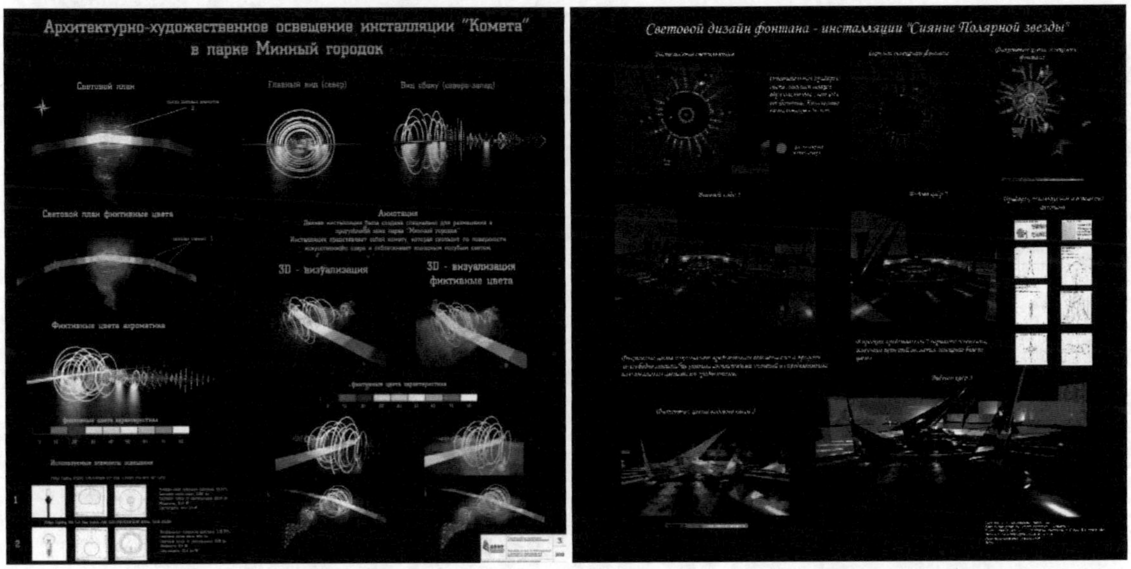

Fig. 2. Blue water reflection and glow, special direction blue light in educational light installation and fountain, in "genius loci" context, op-art and psychology identity.

1.1.3 Modeling of media facade

Modern trends in architecture and design actively use interactive, network and computer technologies. Architecture becomes the background for the broadcasting of certain media content. Buildings and structures acquire a second visual envelope – a media facade, which allows the daytime parameters of the architectural object to be transformed into displays of advertisements and other visual images at night. A media facade is a large-scale display, which consists, as a rule, of LED modules. However, today media facades acquire a variety of artistic and technical forms. The media facades, for example, also can be applied to video-mapping – the projection of content on buildings and structures. The purpose of the practical work is to study the artistic, lighting technical features and means, the methods of creating media facades with use of LED, information, network and wireless technologies, taking into account also the optical and psychological effects and illusions generated by artificial light.

Previously studied analogues of media facades revealed their typology in accordance with the technical device and the use of LEDs in their construction. Artistic methods of media facade content are based on the use of light graphic or visuals, animations. Light sources can also create raster or point animation, or a static image. The features of the media facade content are determined by the power of the light projection or the technology of the LED monitors. According to the projection method, the lamps can illuminate the facade of the building or exhibit interior light passing through the glass facade. Media facades may also not contain light elements. In such cases, their mechanical parts, repeatedly replicated on the plane of the facade of the building, form a kind of mechanical mutable forms. [5, 6]

1.1.4 Modeling the light image of building or architectural ensemble

The night visual image of a building or architectural ensemble is built up through local illumination or general flood lighting. In the first case, spot lights are placed on the building, which can detect certain details, for example, columns, pilasters, fragments of walls, porticos or other architectural elements. This creates light tectonics and a certain light rhythm. Total flood lighting of the building increases the light scale. Lighting several nearby buildings, for example, the architectural ensemble of a historic street can form a light ensemble. The purpose of the practical work: the formation of the light ensemble of a historic street; application of modern media and lighting technologies, lighting systems and LED light sources.

Simulation of architectural ensemble light form consists of individual facade light models of buildings, connected in a single complex by light-composite lighting techniques. Pre-executed also are contour, color models, schemes of arrangement of lighting installations with a designation of beams direction. With the help of brightness programming (regulation of maximum brightness and illumination), the dominant volumes of the most significant architectural objects, which form the city's quarters, are illuminated, whereas intermediate objects form the local non-main illumination. Revealing architectural dominants, modeling and arrangement of maximum and minimum brightnesses of illuminated buildings are done with light revealing the depth and planning of the historical environment and space of the street. Complex plastic facades of historic buildings are emphasized by local color and common flood light. Different rays are used. The light silhouette of the buildings' facades and forged elements of the parapets and balcony fences (reception of the contre-jour), the light rhythm of the facades' plastic elements are revealed. A light accentuation of axial forms (arches, niches, windows, pediments, porticos), domed corner elements of the buildings' composition are created. [2] When modeling the light image of a unique building, shown in Fig. 3, the light graphics associated with sea waves are applied: curvilinear point drawing, cold light (P. Malineva, Ja. Nipunova). These light elements contain a symbolic link to the name of the building "Ocean" – a cinema is located in the embankment of a seaside city, and elements of the identity of "genius loci".

Fig. 3. Methods of light modeling – blue glow, light structuring of volume in unique architectural object.

1.1.5 Modeling of city pedestrian lightspaces

In the theory of modern light urbanism, two main types of light spaces are distinguished: transport, and pedestrian. In the city's transport spaces, more attention is devoted to the road utilitarian illumination which is determined by the visibility parameters for drivers with high speed in night conditions. At the same time, the current concept of the new urbanism, containing a number of basic principles, such as pedestrian accessibility, multifunctionality, quality of life and others, places the pedestrian in a priority position in the urban life system. Herewith, the aesthetics and ergonomics of the light environment, its filling with small light forms, light information and advertising, modern lights acquire a great importance. In turn, the pedestrian light spaces can be divided into spaces of communication, movement and recreation by the nature of the behavior and speed of the pedestrians' movement. Hence, different light parameters of the environment, depend on the conditions of visual perception and visual connections, the nature of people's behavior, and the urban structure. Comfortable and chamber lighting is used in the rest areas. The traffic spaces (sidewalks) are parallel to the roads, but the lighting is largely on the pedestrians in such spaces. Spaces of communication, as the most important planning elements of the city, can be distinguished by bright and neutral-white light, high level of illumination, special light-composition techniques, and a system of light signs and visual communications. This practical task has a complex nature. It can generalize the development of previous tasks and include techniques of light composition, new light installations and media facades, light ensembles and dominants. The goal of the practical work is to create a harmonious, artistically expressive, comfortable and safe light environment of a city's pedestrian area, the use of modern media and lighting technologies, lighting systems and light sources.

Modeling the pedestrian space supposes initial functional zoning with the goal of determining the qualitative (chromaticity of light, density and light field nature, light dynamics) and quantitative (brightness and illumination level) parameters of the light environment. In the process of zoning pedestrian spaces the light spaces are divided into that of communication, movement and recreation, for which the appropriate types of lamps are chosen: architectural, landscape, road-pedestrian and decorative purposes. The media surfaces, light installations, light sculptures, previously created in other practical works are used in pedestrian spaces. Light-spatial depth is achieved by the methods of light panorama. The functional indexes of the environment – homogeneity of illumination with specified color temperature, brightness and illumination level, and figurative-artistic characteristics – creation and realization of light composition effects, adjusted psychoemotional atmosphere of comfort, safety and rest, are achieved when modeling artificial light. Blue glow of the plankton of the sea refers to the images of water, wave, sea depth, bottomlessness. The modeling of light-form receptions associatively constitutes stable psychological connections and creative thinking, which cause figurative associative thinking in the context of creative identity. [2, 7-9]

Figure 4 presents practical work on the formation of the light environment of the coastal space of the city Vladivostok – the embankment. The image on the left shows the project "Architectural and artistic illumination of Vladivostok Sports Harbor" (E. Kiseleva). The main idea of the project is the development and application of wind energy in the light installations and the creation of uniform horizontal illumination. The design of the lamp includes a wind turbine (one meter diameter), which consists of six working blades. Wind-generated energy is integrated in the accumulator. Flashlights can be used as a power battery and electricity. The lights are charged for lighting walkways in the evening. These light units and a luminous flux are produced from a central control. In the image to the right – the project "Designing architectural and artistic illumination of Vladivostok Sports waterfront "Bioluminescence of the sea" (A. Voroncova). The main idea of this project is to imitate the bioluminescent glow of marine organisms in order to create a bright image of the Sports waterfront attractive for visitors in the evening. This decorative lighting will create a special atmosphere of the coast, making a walk along the waterfront more enjoyable, especially on foggy days. The project includes conceptual design lamps, and a list of recommended equipment. Feature of the project is small LED elements embedded in the pavement, which gradually light up and fade in a certain rhythm, simulating the glow of plankton in the water.

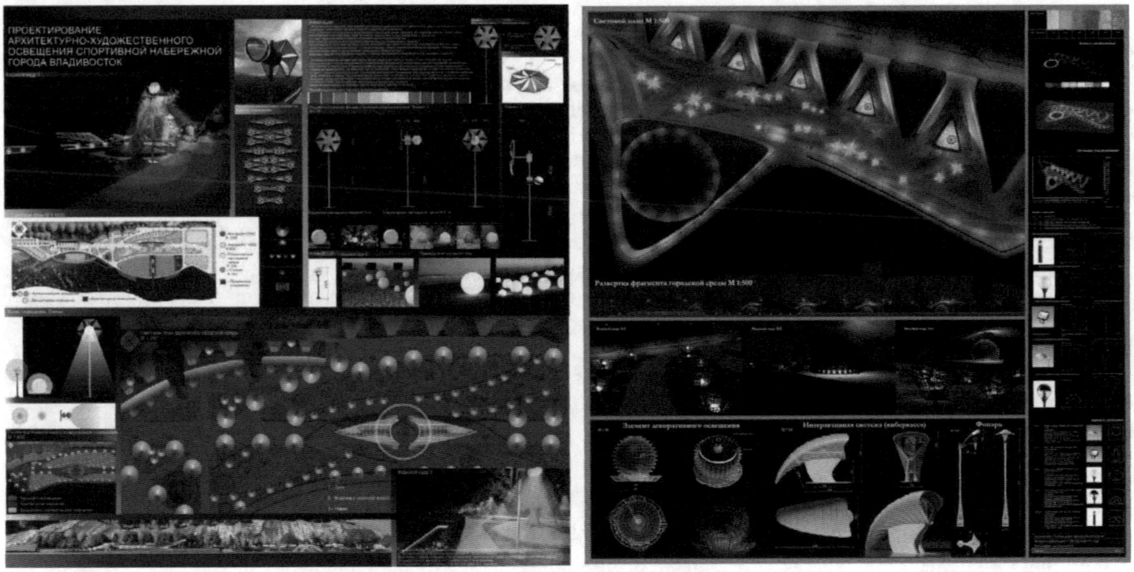

Fig. 4. Modeling and using of seawater images in lighting effects of the practical works. Formation of "genius loci" in architectural-light environment of the Vladivostok embankments.

1.2 Methods of the educational complex

1.2.1 Variationality

The choice and performance of a particular assignment depends on the preliminary design of the day-time architectural environment and the goals and tasks of individual preference. This determines the principle of variation in the educational complex. The smoothness of the educational process consists of the sequential acquaintance with the works of optical art, the trends in the world of light design and new forms in the urban environment, the means of virtual design, the achievements of lighting technology and psychology.

1.2.2 Complementarity

The light techniques of each practical work are mutually complementary. They can be used and supplemented in any practical work. Elements and receptions of light design worked out in every practical work can be used in other practical works. For example, the techniques of light composition are used in the design of light architectural ensemble and object; media facades are used in the design of a fragment of the light environment of a pedestrian space or an architectural object.

1.2.3 The principle of 3 models

The principle of three models includes the stage of creating a light image of an object or a form, which are depicted in the form of sketch drawings. Graphic model is preliminarily formed – creating a contour drawing of an object. This project stage fixes the proportional and compositional features of the object. Architectural rhythm, plastic, tectonics are then analyzed. Following that, the color (reproduction of the color of the object) and the light model are formed. The second stage is the creation of light model, which is creation of the light architecture of the object, taking into account its color parameters and architectural plastics. This stage involves the creation of a light rhythm of the elements of the facade's plastic, installation, composition and identification of tectonics. Points for placing luminaires of local or general flood lighting are marked. Herewith, the techniques of light composition can be used. The basic principles of lighting for a particular object, which take into account the contour pattern, proportional and compositional features, rhythm, plastic, tectonics, color, light and shape silhouette, are formulated.
The means of modeling the light environment are computer graphics, as well as a sketch with artistic visual means – dark paper and pastel. Means of designing the light environment are computer modeling, in which the values of illumination or brightness are checked in the theoretical environment, and the distribution and nature of artificial light, brightness fields and contrasts are simulated. The creation of a light composition also includes a prototyping process, in which miniature color diode light sources, light-transmitting and reflective materials are used.

2 Results of educational-practical works

The light composition in the lighting design is defined as a form consisting of a series of transparent and opaque elements, the main idea of which is manifested when using an artificial light source. Simultaneously, it is characterized by the dynamics or static of the light effect. As a result of the educational process, means of light composition have been developed. These include: specular, diffuse and mixed reflection and its structural capabilities, contrast (shadow), transmission of light, and chromaticity. Simultaneously, the mechanism of the formation and use of psychological skills, associations, motility and memory in using special techniques in light form, composition, and in the spaces of the embankments of the city was discovered. For example, wavy lines - light graphics, blue light, gradients of brightness, vanishing and flickering blue water light projected onto the foil light, are elements that make up the light composition which are associated with sea waves, a sea city. Such a light composition can be expressed in objects of the Vladivostok embankments, referring to the local-geographical identity. Thus, the objects of the light design acquire a different meaning, evoking and referring to the figurative memory and spirit of the place, which resides in all the seaside cities in general. Light techniques transform the object and inscribe it into the environment and approximate its sense of finding and matching the image of the place.

The design of the media facade is conditioned by the development of LED technologies and the increase of luminous flux of the projection devices [5, 6]. Modern trends in the technical and artistic means of media facades acquire a variety of artistic and technical forms, to which can also be attributed video-mapping. Many of the light techniques and artistic form of the light composition worked out by the students resemble a light installation in miniature [4].

The night visual image of a building or architectural ensemble is built by local illumination or general flood lighting. In the first case spotlights soffits, which can reveal architectural details, are placed on the building. Total flood lighting of the building increases the light scale. The lighting of several nearby buildings of a historic street can form a light ensemble. The logic of lighting historical objects or buildings in the style of eclecticism, historicism, postmodernism with complex facade plasticity dictates the identification of light tectonics.

In the night embankment spaces, light forms a background and "edges" [7]. It is a planning and spatial atmospheric design tool that identifies road and transport structures and boundaries, landscape and plant elements. It is also a warning component [9]. Light is an active element of environmental forms and constructions and reproduces the effects of light composition.

When modeling lighting projects, we came to the conclusion that in light design, the volume-spatial composition of an architectural object determines the techniques of light composition, and the contextuality of their use in accordance with the spirit and identity of the place, as evidenced by the methodology and project-methodological practice in creating a light image of the object. Objects themselves in many ways set the choice of lighting techniques. The development of light composition is also aimed at developing the skills of invention and fantasy of light techniques, which then find expression in objects of the environment and architecture, in new light images.

3 New technologies in modeling the city's artificial light environment

3.1 Light structural elements as modeling units in the urban environment

Kevin Lynch's theoretical works (1960) in the field of image formation of a city are taken into account in light modeling from the point of view of the methodology of the planning structure of the city. He defined five structural elements: landmarks, paths, nodes, borders and districts [7]. Each of these elements and their combination in light-composition interpretation – certain fragments of the urban environment, buildings or architectural ensembles, can be highlighted with certain light-composition techniques or light stimulus. The universality of the structural theory is expressed in the fact that it can be applied to various spaces of the city, visually perceived directly by man. At the same time, certain emotional characteristics of the environment are created, its atmosphericity is achieved.

Intuitive subconscious following of a person to the bright spaces in the evening, to the direction of light forms as landmarks, paths, nodes, boundaries, areas and dominants, which is determined by the physiological mechanisms of visual transmission of light signal, specifies a certain program, and trajectory of motion. This is the psychological meaning of the light stimulus – to encourage activity in the night space of the city. The ways of urban displacement, the acquisition of cognitive and emotional-sensory reactions, the establishment of visual and psychological connections in the urban environment by means of recognizing the light stimulus, signs, light fields, the planning structure of the city and its elements, form certain atmospheric environments of the city; and the light forms execute the function of a light guide. At the same time, the process of visual perception has an individual and subjective character. [2, 10, 11]

3.2 Neuro, wireless, bioluminescent technologies and light forms in urban environment modeling

The impact of artificial light in psychological processes is expressed in its ability to form a spatio-temporal distribution of light stimulus on the retina of the eye, send electrical and neurochemical signals further to the visual regions of the brain, and cause imaginative thought processes and associations. In this case, neurostimulants are combinations of light stimulus in light form or light composition.

With the help of light form, it brings the possibility to create special light techniques that play the role of neurostimulators and neuroprogrammers, thus allowing emotional states to be set with the help of new light technologies and tools. Light stimulus can create a positive mood and have a certain therapeutic and psychological effect on a person. By stimulus, light effects are the structural parts of the light form. Thus, a psychological reconstruction and adjustment of emotional settings take place in the night city space with the help of light stimulus and the effects in the light composition. The introduction of light installations, media facades, light sculptures and small architectural forms into the urban environment is a means of excitation of neuroprocesses, and the forms themselves are neurostimulants.

Artificial light technologies change the biological rhythms of a person in a modern city. The "infinity of the day" is formed taking into account the predominance of the negative impact of the blue spectrum of radiation in LED technologies. Continuity of artificial light technologies, density and quality of the light flow transform the volume and spatial structure of the city into a virtual structure of visual landmarks, dominants, accents and background. The introduction of sensors, recorders, artificial intelligence, big data technology substantially extends the psychological nature of the stimulus effect of the light form and its techniques, which are, as it were, technical and artificial continuation of human neural channels (neuroconductors). A person turns into a consumer of light urban information in the form of images of light architecture, advertising, signs, and navigators. Urban processes are increasingly being programmed and determined by sensory technologies, and residents have been able to actively participate in this chaos of technology and urban fabric with the help of smartphones. At the same time, such interaction raises questions of visual and psychological ecology, and the creation of favorable psycho-emotional living conditions in the urban environment. Another example of the interaction of nature, man and light is the bioluminescent instrumentation – the generation of light, taking into account the electrochemical processes occurring in living organisms. There is a need for an in-depth further study of the physico-chemical mechanisms of bioluminescence, its biological basis, and their possible practical application in the practice of environmental modeling and the creation of special light techniques. [12-14]

4 Conclusions and prospects of educational technologies in light design

4.1 Main conclusions

Images of new art and technological innovations are short-lived. Media facades, light installations and their technical equipment depend on the parameters of light sources and current art trends, and their meaning. Content changes even more rapidly in the unstable conditions of the modern city.

The methods of projecting light, setting special artistic tasks, revealing the building's tectonic system using artificial light lead to a typological convergence of the light form of the building's facade (light architecture), media facade, light projection and video mapping.

The methodological accents of the educational complex are expressed in a preliminary study of the techniques of optical art, in which works of the light elements or special lighting effects are initially laid and prototypes of the light composition have been constructed. In the process of creating a light composition, a certain number of light techniques are developed. The students studied modern trends in art, the visual series of which allows to develop abstract thinking, expand memory, and invent individual methods of lighting.

The peculiarities of the methodology of this training complex are that for the first time the stages (models), variability (choice of medium in daylight forms for light projection) and complementarity (universality and combination of light techniques for various environmental forms) are proposed in the educational and practical design of the light environment by means of computer simulation.)

The methodological results of the practical work also show that techniques and means, as well as structural combinations of light techniques, help express the light image of buildings, develop and consolidate the student's skills of creating memorable images of the "genius loci", which in turn help express psychological, personal and geographical identity, continuity and identity in optical art. The achieved results show especially in the light composition that psychological and cultural memory is clearly manifested through many stages of development in art. Some techniques of light composition are based on the works of Laszlo Moholy-Nagy [15] and the Bauhaus school as a whole [16]. In the works of students there is a conscious use of forms of optical art. In our opinion, there is a certain temporary identity and continuity in design and art.

4.2 Prospects of educational technologies in light design and modeling

Modern lighting design is transformed into a tool for managing the psychological state and the mood of a urban person. This leads to the neuroprogramming the human consciousness and its behavior. Modern lighting contributes to the transformation of the environment and urban life, largely due to the use of new technical means. But modern visual art offers a wide range of artistic and visual forms. Practical tasks for light-colored modeling of the urban environment reflect the synthesis of new technologies and modern visual art, at the junction of which new environmental forms are formed. Media facades, light installations and their technical equipment depend on the parameters of light sources and actual art techniques, and their content and meaning. Content changes even more rapidly in the unstable conditions of the modern city. Preliminary study of prototypes helps to freely use the means of light design and navigate in the aesthetic directions of contemporary art, which ultimately contributes to the creation of modern and relevant light environment of the city.

The result of the educational complex is the means of light composition: mirror, diffuse and mixed reflection and its structural capabilities, contrast (shadow), radioscopy or transmission of light, and chromaticity. In the embankment spaces, light creates "edges". It is a planning and spatial atmospheric means of designing town-planning units. It identifies road-transport structures and borders, landscape and plant elements; and is a signal and warning component. Light is an active element of environmental forms and reproduces techniques of light composition, as well as compositional logic which defines and determines the choice of various techniques of light composition.

Some practical tasks are built on the basis of the town-planning structure, which includes various public pedestrian areas of the city – embankments, central historical streets and squares. For example, in one of the practical works it is necessary to project a light environment of pedestrian space, use lamps or light devices offered by well-known companies. In any case, the main goal of light modeling is to create a harmonious, safe and artistically expressive light environment that combines modern medium and light technologies. At the same time, light-modeling techniques can be expanded; their purpose can be diverse and extensive while simultaneously achieving the necessary image-visual effects.

References

1. M. Holzhey, *Victor Vasarely. 1906–1997. Pure Vision* (Tashen, Köln, 2005)
2. N. I. Shchepetkov, *Light design of the city* (Architecture – S, Moscow, 2006)
3. A. V. Efimov, *Color + form. The Art of 20-21 centuries (painting, sculpture, installation, land art, digital art* (BooksMArt, Moscow, 2014)
4. *Italian Zero & avantgarde '60s* (Silvana Editoriale Spa, Cinisello Balsamo, Milano, 2011)
5. *Ag4. Media Fasades* (Published and distributed worldwide by daab gmbh, 2006)

6. M. H. Haeusler, *Media Facades. History, Technology, Content* (Leibfarth & Schwarz GmbH & Co.KG, Ludwigsburg, 2009)
7. K. Lynch, *The Image of the City* (The MIT Press, 1960)
8. J. Jacobs, *The Death and Life of Great American Cities* (Vintage, 1992)
9. R. Narboni, *Lighting the Landscape. Art Design Technologies* (Brikhäuser – Publishers for Architecture, 2004)
10. G. Debord, *The Society of the Spectacle* (Annotated Edition, Bureau of Public Secrets, 2014)
11. C. Ellard, *Places of The Heart. The Psychogeography of Everyday Life* (Bellevue Literary Press, New York, 2015)
12. E. Kandel, *The Age of Insight: The Quest to Understand the Unconscious in Art, Mind, and Brain, from Vienna 1900 to the Present* (Random House, 2012)
13. W. J. Mitchell, *Me++: The Cyborg Self and the Networked City* (The MIT Press, 2004)
14. S. Stossel, *My Age of Anxiety: Fear, Hope, Dread, and the Search for Peace of Mind* (Knopf, 2014)
15. L. Moholy-Nagy, *Telehor* (Ad Marginem Press, 2014)
16. R. Goldberg, *Performance Art From Futurism to the Present* (Thames & Hadson, 2011)

AUTHOR INDEX